EXPLORING
THE OLD NORTH END
NEIGHBORHOOD OF
COLORADO SPRINGS

A GUIDE TO ITS HISTORY & ARCHITECTURE

Published by the Old North End Neighborhood (ONEN)

P.O. Box 8185

Colorado Springs, CO 80933-8185

oldnorthend.org

Designed by CoPilot Creative, Colorado Springs, CO

Printed by Fittje Brothers Printing Company, Colorado Springs, CO

The authors would like to thank the following people and organizations for their support and assistance in the production of this book:

The Old North End Neighborhood (ONEN) Board; the ONEN Historic Preservation Committee; the ONEN Book Sub-Committee (Pat Doyle, Susan Darby, Terry Darby, and Judith Finley); the Historic Preservation Alliance of Colorado Springs; Elizabeth Blackwell at the State Historical Fund; the staff of Special Collections at Pikes Peak Library District; the staff of Special Collections at Tutt Library at Colorado College; Stephen Fischer and Bill Stookey at the El Paso County Assessor's Office; Allison Wendler; and Elaine Freed.

All contemporary photographs by Jennifer Wendler Lovell, 2010.

Front Cover Photograph: *Letitia Finn pushing her carriage, c. 1910. The houses in the background are 1627 and 1621 N. Nevada Avenue. (Courtesy Special Collections, Pikes Peak Library District. Image 229-6006.)*

Back Cover Photograph: *The 1700 block of N. Nevada Avenue, looking south, 1927. (Photograph by Harry L. Standley, courtesy Special Collections, Pikes Peak Library District. Image 102-10384.)*

Table Of Contents

Foreword 7

A History of the Old North End Neighborhood 9

The Architecture of the Old North End Neighborhood 23

Architectural Style Guide 29

Walking Tours of the Old North End Neighborhood
Tour 1- Monument Valley Park Area 46
Tour 2- Wood Avenue 58
Tour 3- N. Cascade Avenue 80
Tour 4- N. Tejon Street 94
Tour 5- N. Nevada Avenue 108
Tour 6- N. Weber Street/N. Wahsatch Avenue 124

Glossary of Terms 141

Index 149

Bibliography 157

Map of the Old North End Neighborhood 161

Foreword

This project was funded in part by a State Historical Fund grant award from History Colorado, the Colorado Historical Society. The Old North End Neighborhood (ONEN) and the Historic Preservation Alliance (HPA) of Colorado Springs provided additional funds.

The intent of this book is to raise awareness of the Old North End neighborhood's distinctive architecture and historical significance and to encourage the preservation of the neighborhood's irreplaceable buildings and historic residential character.

In choosing the areas of the neighborhood to feature on the walking tours, several considerations were important. Because the tours needed to be a reasonable walking distance, each tour was planned to be a distance of less than 1.5 miles. In addition, each tour begins at or near Uintah Street, as this is where the neighborhood's earliest concentrated development began. The northern portion of the neighborhood could not be included in the tours for these reasons. However, readers are encouraged to explore the northern blocks of the neighborhood, as they are filled with many architectural gems.

Properties were selected for the walking tours based on the architecture, history, and location of the house. All of the historic architectural styles in the neighborhood are represented in the walking tours, and those houses that best exemplify those styles were chosen. When possible, those houses with a high degree of architectural integrity were selected. This included houses that had most of their original materials intact and had either no additions or minimal, architecturally compatible additions. A number of houses have also been featured due to their association with historically significant residents or prominent architects. In addition, an effort was made to space the featured houses at regular intervals throughout each of the walking tours.

A History Of
The Old North End
Neighborhood

by Robert D. Loevy

Early Stirrings

As a part of a concept in one man's mind, the Old North End neighborhood came into existence on July 27, 1869. On that day, William Jackson Palmer first rode into a spectacular red rock area just to the north of Colorado City, Colorado Territory. Even at that early date, the area was known as the Garden of the Gods.

Palmer had been a general in the Union Army during the Civil War. A railroad builder, he had come to the Garden of the Gods while surveying a railroad route from Kansas City to Denver.

*William Jackson Palmer
(Courtesy Special Collections, Pikes Peak Library District. Image 001-375.)*

General Palmer described the area, which had glorious views of 14,000-foot-high Pike's Peak, as "enticing." He noted its potential to become a "famous resort." At that moment, General Palmer resolved to build a new city on a flat plain located east of the Garden of the Gods. The name of the new city was Colorado Springs.

"My theory for this place," General Palmer wrote, "is that it should be made the most attractive place for homes in the West." It thus is clear that William Jackson Palmer wanted his new city to include fine residential areas. The Old North End is one of a number of neighborhoods in Colorado Springs that meets General Palmer's dictum of being "the most attractive place for homes in the West."

Colorado College

Colorado Springs was founded on July 31, 1871. The first stake was driven at the corner of Pike's Peak Avenue and Cascade Avenue, which was to become the center of the downtown area. Ten blocks north of the first stake, near the corner of Cache La Poudre Street and Cascade Avenue, General Palmer set aside more than 20 acres of land for a college or university.

Colorado College, Cutler Hall, c. 1880.
(Courtesy Special Collections, Pikes Peak Library District. Image 001-113.)

On that site, in 1874, Colorado College was founded. It was to become a small, co-educational liberal arts college of the New England type.

The land to the north of the college would subsequently become the Old North End of Colorado Springs. Throughout the 1870s and 1880s, however, there was little recorded activity on this land.

Gold!

Gold was first discovered in what later became Colorado in 1858. The resulting gold rush attracted thousands of people to the future state, but not many of them came to the area around Colorado Springs. The successful gold mining sites in Colorado were mainly to the west and north of Denver at a considerable distance from Colorado Springs.

Many prospectors had attempted to find gold on Pike's Peak, the high Rocky Mountain to the west of Colorado Springs that was rapidly becoming the best-known mountain in the United States. In 1890, a ne'er-do-well cowboy named Robert Womack did some prospecting for precious metals. While digging next to the banks of a stream called Cripple Creek, Bob Womack dug out some ore samples that contained real gold. He later sold his claim for a relatively small amount of money, but other men hurried up to Cripple Creek and turned the area into a booming gold mining district.

By 1892, over $500,000 in gold had been mined in Cripple Creek and a neighboring gold camp at Victor, Colorado. Production soared to $7 million in gold by 1896. Soon Cripple Creek and Victor were generating the largest mining profits in Colorado history.

Cripple Creek and Victor rapidly became rough, roaring, and bawdy mining camps. Both were located at around 10,000 feet of elevation and had few amenities. Only 40 miles away, at first by road and then by three different railroads, sat the city of Colorado Springs, the quiet community that General Palmer had founded to be a city of comfort and grace.

Quite naturally, most of the men who rushed to Cripple Creek and Victor to make money in this latest gold boom did not want to build their homes and locate their families in these high-elevation mining camps. They elected instead to move to Colorado Springs and only go up to Cripple Creek and Victor when business required it. The result was a phenomenal residential boom in Colorado Springs. From 1890 to 1900, the population more than doubled in General Palmer's little "resort" in the Rocky Mountains.

The Old North End Boom

The Cripple Creek and Victor gold mines thus brought a large group of newly-wealthy people to Colorado Springs. Some of them were mine owners who "struck it rich" on the southwest slopes of Pike's Peak and became instant millionaires. Many others,

The northwest corner of Uintah Street and Cascade Avenue, c. 1895
(Courtesy Special Collections, Tutt Library, Colorado College, Colorado Springs, Colorado.)

however, were middle-class beneficiaries of the Cripple Creek and Victor gold boom. They were stock traders, or mining company office managers, or merchants who sold supplies and services to the mining companies.

These people needed a place to live, and the timing was just right for the Old North End. Many of these newcomers to Colorado Springs, and some old-timers too, bought lots on the land north of Colorado College. The millionaires built grand mansions. The middle class built large houses on long lots.

It was, in essence, this 1890s building boom that created the unified architectural character of much of the Old North End. Thanks to the money being made from the Cripple Creek and Victor gold mines, a large number of homes were built in the Old North End in a relatively short period of time. These homes all reflected late 19th Century and early 20th Century building styles. Most of the older homes in the Old North End that are prized so highly were constructed between 1890 and 1910, the Cripple Creek and Victor boom years.

Penrose Hospital

Tuberculosis and other pulmonary diseases were a major health problem in the United States in the late 19th and early 20th centuries. One of the treatments for such lung ailments was for patients to move to a high elevation in the Rocky Mountains, where the cool, dry air often retarded the development of such diseases. A popular place for tuberculosis patients to come was Colorado Springs, which has an elevation of around 6,000 feet.

A prominent tuberculosis sanitorium in Colorado Springs was Glockner Hospital, located on North Cascade Avenue in the northern part of the Old North End. Founded in 1890, the hospital was surrounded by the invalid tents in which "consumption" patients dwelled in an effort to expose themselves to as much outdoor air and sunshine as possible.

Glockner Hospital, c. 1950
(Photograph by James and Helen McCaffery, courtesy Special Collections, Pikes Peak Library District. Image 266-10135.)

Glockner Hospital was named in memory of Albert Glockner, who had come to Colorado Springs from Pittsburgh, Pennsylvania, in search of a cure for his tuberculosis. Following his death in 1888, his wife Marie decided to build the sanitorium in his honor. The hospital was operated for several years by Mrs. Glockner, but she later turned control over to the Sisters of Charity of Cincinnati, Ohio. Over the years, the institution evolved into Penrose Hospital, one of the leading hospitals in Colorado Springs.

The hospital had a major impact on the development of the Old North End. Doctors and other high-income medical personnel who worked at the hospital began buying homes in the surrounding neighborhood. As a result, medical doctors and their families became a major presence in the Old North End, often owning and living in a number of the larger and more prestigious homes.

Monument Valley Park

In 1901, General William Jackson Palmer, the founder of Colorado Springs, began to liquidate his remaining interests in the railroad industry and went into retirement. Thereafter, he devoted his time, his affection, and a significant portion of his personal fortune to improving Colorado Springs.

Monument Creek runs through Colorado Springs in a north-to-south direction through the center of the city. As it does so, a portion of the creek forms the western boundary of the Old North End. General Palmer and his consulting engineer, E. C. Van Diest, turned Monument Creek and the lands surrounding it into Monument Valley Park.

Monument Valley Park, c. 1915
(Courtesy Special Collections, Pikes Peak Library District. Image 102-2249.)

After purchasing the necessary acreages, Palmer had the park landscaped, creating delightful walking paths, rustic bridges, lakes, and comfortable benches on which to sit and enjoy the wonders of nature in an urban park setting.

Monument Valley Park stretched all the way from downtown Colorado Springs, past the Colorado College campus, and then north along the west side of the Old North End. Approximately 50 percent of the new park was immediately adjacent to the Old North End, thus becoming a major addition to the quality of life in the neighborhood. Residents of the area could easily walk or bicycle to the park and enjoy its many amenities. As the years went by, many new homes were constructed in the Old North End on lands that bordered on, and were enhanced by, the beauties and pleasures of Monument Valley Park.

The park opened to public use in 1907. It soon became home to a variety of songbirds, as well as a number of other wild animals, including red foxes. Monument Valley Park is enjoyed by people from the entire community of

Colorado Springs. Joggers, bicyclists, volleyball players, and softball players come in large numbers to join Old North Enders in experiencing the many pleasures of Monument Valley Park.

The North Tejon Street Trolley

Electric streetcars came to Colorado Springs toward the end of the 19th Century. One streetcar company operated on North Tejon Street and proposed building its tracks right through the middle of Colorado College. William Frederick Slocum, the president of the college, was appalled at the prospect of trolley cars clanging their way through the very center of the campus. President Slocum prevailed on General Palmer to join him in opposing the plan of the streetcar company to bisect the Colorado College campus with trolley tracks and noisy trolley cars.

The City Council of Colorado Springs sided with President Slocum and General Palmer. The trolley company was forced to route its tracks around the Colorado College campus. The trolley went east to Nevada Avenue on Cache La Poudre Street, then turned north on Nevada Avenue to

Trolley cars, c. 1899–1901
(Photograph by F. P. Stevens, courtesy Special Collections, Pikes Peak Library District. Image 005-4178.)

Uintah Street. Next the trolley turned west on Uintah Street before resuming its northward trip up Tejon Street, running northward through the Old North End.

To make certain that Tejon Street and its trolley cars could never run through the college campus, Colorado College proceeded to construct Palmer Hall, a major classroom and laboratory building. The 1904 building was located right at the spot where Tejon Street would come through the campus. There was speculation, never substantiated, that General Palmer made an anonymous contribution of $100,000 for the construction of Palmer Hall so that Tejon Street would be permanently blocked.

The closing of Tejon Street at the Colorado College campus had an important effect on the development of the Old North End. It prevented Tejon Street, where it runs through the Old North End, from becoming a heavily-trafficked street. Automobile drivers could not use this route to drive from the northern part of Colorado Springs into the downtown area. The result was that Tejon Street, despite having the streetcar line, became one of the quieter streets in the Old North End where automobile noise and congestion were concerned.

The streetcar line, which probably was not all that noisy, added to the ambiance of the Old North End in the early years of the 20th Century. Because the neighborhood runs predominantly on a north/south axis, most of the homes were within easy walking distance of the Tejon Street trolley cars. Residents who were employed downtown could ride the trolley to and from work. The trolley could also be used for shopping trips downtown and for high school students to ride to Colorado Springs High School, which was located at Platte and Nevada avenues.

The Great Depression of the early 1930s put an end to streetcar service in Colorado Springs. The trolleys were replaced by buses. The North Tejon Street bus faithfully followed the route of the old trolley cars, bypassing Colorado College by jogging over to Nevada Avenue. In the early 1970s, after the City of Colorado Springs took over the bus service, the buses were removed from Tejon Street and began running straight through to downtown on North Cascade Avenue.

Tejon Street is not the only north-south street in the Old North End, however, that benefits from being closed at Colorado College. Wood Avenue extends northward only from Uintah Street. Because General Palmer gave Colorado College all the land west of Cascade Avenue extending to Monument Creek, it was impossible for Wood Avenue to be connected to downtown Colorado Springs. This reduced the amount of automobile traffic being carried on Wood Avenue.

Landscaped Medians

One of the most significant and important developments in the history of the Old North End was the building and planting of the landscaped street medians in the center of Wood, Cascade, Nevada, and Wahsatch avenues. Many persons in Colorado Springs believe that General Palmer put in the landscaped medians, but that is not quite the case. General Palmer provided the wide main streets in which the landscaped medians are located, but the raised and planted medians were the result of the City Beautiful movement of the early 20th Century.

The City Beautiful movement, as its name implies, was a national effort to improve and beautify the appearance of cities, both major and minor, throughout the United States. The movement resulted in the creation of heavily landscaped parks in American cities and the construction of a large

Median on Nevada Avenue, c. 1916
(Photograph by Photo Craft Shop, courtesy Special Collections, Pikes Peak Library District. Image 001-5021.)

number of public buildings, such as art museums, which were often fashioned in white marble to look like Greek and Roman buildings of antiquity. It was inevitable that the City Beautiful movement would reach Colorado Springs.

City leaders hired noted urban planner Charles Mulford Robinson to come to Colorado Springs, survey the city, and make recommendations for civic beautification. The principal recommendation in the report was to raise the medians in the major streets and landscape them with trees, shrubbery, flowers, and green grass. The recommendation was implemented, and almost one-third of the landscaped street medians created were in the Old North End.

A variety of landscaping styles were used in the new medians, thereby differentiating the look of one street from another. North Nevada Avenue was planted with a long, stately, double-row of leaf trees (deciduous trees), giving the street a particularly verdant look in the summertime.

On Wood, Cascade, and Wahsatch avenues, however, a more varied approach was taken, with evergreen trees (coniferous trees) alternating with leaf trees and more emphasis on shrubbery and flowerbeds. A number of crabapple trees, with lovely pink flowers, and lilac trees, with blue and purple hues, help to make Wood, Cascade, and Wahsatch avenues a riot of blossoming color during the early spring.

Wood Avenue presents something of an unusual case. Only two blocks of Wood Avenue, from Uintah Street to Columbia Street, have a landscaped median. One charming feature in those two blocks is the presence of ornate, cast iron streetlights with a distinctly Victorian look. These two blocks are the old Millionaires' Row created by the Cripple Creek and Victor gold boom.

"Millionaires' Row" on Wood Avenue, c. 1910
(Courtesy Special Collections, Tutt Library, Colorado College, Colorado Springs, Colorado.)

North of Columbia Street, Wood Avenue loses its landscaped medians but gains a feature almost as valuable. Large areas filled with trees and grass were placed between the sidewalk and the street curb, giving the street almost as lush a look in the summertime as if it had a landscaped median.

In the Old North End, the landscaped medians are the perfect complement to the historic homes found on the major avenues that traverse the neighborhood. Residents proved as committed to preserving those landscaped medians as they were to maintaining the historical appearance of the homes.

Goodbye Gold Boom

By the early 1920s, the great gold boom at Cripple Creek and Victor had begun to wane. There was still plenty of gold in the ground. The problem was that the U.S. Government would not pay enough for the gold to make it worthwhile to dig it out of the earth. The market price of gold slowly dropped to the point where it cost more to mine the gold than the price for which it could be sold.

The decline of gold mining at Cripple and Victor had a depressing economic effect on Colorado Springs. The glory days were over. The big money that helped to build those beautiful Victorian homes in the Old North End was no longer flowing into the city. During the 1920s and the 1930s, Colorado Springs and the Old North End became relatively quiet places. There was very little population growth in the city and a greatly reduced rate of housing construction. The 30-year era, from 1890 to 1920, of building large homes in the Old North End had come to an end.

The lack of boisterous economic activity in Colorado Springs during the two decades of the 1920s and the 1930s actually helped to preserve the historic character of the Old North End. If the city had continued to grow in population, automobile traffic would have increased on Cascade, Nevada, Weber, and Wahsatch avenues. That in turn would have increased the pressure to convert the larger houses on those streets to apartments and, perhaps, commercial businesses. This would have occurred at a time when there was no Old North End Neighborhood association to oppose and resist such conversions to multi-family dwellings and street-front shops and stores.

World War Two And The Old North End

The outbreak of World War Two completely changed the economic situation in Colorado Springs. The United States Government began building and operating a number of major military facilities in and near the city. One was Fort Carson, a large U.S. Army training facility for mechanized warfare. Another was Peterson Field, an Army Air Corps base for training bomber pilots.

During World War Two, there was an acute housing shortage in Colorado Springs. One result was the creation of a number of basement and garage apartments in some of the larger homes in the Old North End. In some cases, entire Victorian homes were converted to apartments to house the large numbers of military personnel who came to Colorado Springs to help win the war.

Once World War Two was over, housing construction resumed in Colorado Springs. Modern homes were built on the vacant lots that still remained in the Old North End. This was particularly true in the western portion of the neighborhood near Monument Valley Park. A number of newer and more modern homes, some of them one-story ranch houses, were constructed in the area around Alamo and Culebra avenues. Portions of the Old North End began to take on somewhat more of an eclectic look where architectural styles were concerned.

The Old North End Neighborhood (ONEN)

In 1955, Penrose Hospital announced plans to build a 14-story hospital building at North Cascade Avenue and Madison Street at the northern edge of the Old North End. The building was going to be the highest building constructed in Colorado Springs up to that time. Although most Old North End residents considered themselves friends and supporters of Penrose Hospital, a number of them questioned the wisdom of putting such a tall building in one of the most beautiful historic neighborhoods in Colorado Springs.

Two residents of the Old North End, Jean Szymanski and Ruth Shaw, organized their neighbors to oppose construction of the new hospital building. Although they lost the battle against the expansion of the hospital, Szymanski and Shaw succeeded at forming the homeowners' association that eventually became the Old North End Neighborhood (ONEN). Jean Szymanski served as president of the organization from 1958 to 1968.

The rapid population growth in Colorado Springs during the late 1960s and early 1970s put a variety of new economic pressures on the Old North End. Traffic increased substantially on Cascade and Nevada avenues. With all those automobiles driving by, some property owners in the neighborhood were tempted to convert their houses into commercial usages, such as arts-and-crafts stores or sidewalk-cafe restaurants. The homeowners' association became the logical organization to resist these compromises to the residential character of the Old North End.

The Old North End mainly employed the zoning laws of Colorado Springs to stop the incursion of commercial uses into the neighborhood. Because most of the Old North End was zoned residential, lobbying the Colorado Springs City Council to strictly enforce the residential zoning codes became the first line of defense for the neighborhood. Beverly Reinitz, president of the association from 1969 to 1975, fought many successful battles to keep small retail stores, office buildings, and multi-family housing projects out of the Old North End.

Beverly Reinitz and others also worked hard to see that West Fontanero Street in the Old North End was not extended across Monument Valley Park and connected to an interchange on Interstate Highway 25. They viewed the potential increase in automobile traffic as highly injurious to the residential character of the neighborhood.

National Register Historic Districts

Robert D. Loevy served as the president of the neighborhood association from 1976 to 1980. In 1976, he drove to Denver and met with officials of the Colorado Historical Society. After Loevy gave a verbal description of the historic character of the neighborhood, state officials agreed to consider the Old North End for classification as a National Register Historic District. Following a tour of the neighborhood by state officials, the application for National Register Historic District status moved forward with official support from the State of Colorado.

An architectural analysis and evaluation of the Old North End was prepared by Elaine Freed, a Colorado Springs historical consultant and a longtime resident of the Old North End. Photographs of the significant homes in the neighborhood were taken by Barbara Sparks, also an Old North Ender. In the early 1980s, a large portion of the Old North End was officially declared a National Register Historic District. It was the first residential area in Colorado Springs to be designated as such.

In February of 1985, a second residential historic district in Colorado Springs was listed on the National Register. The North Weber-Wahsatch National Register Historic District extended northward along Weber Street from just north of downtown Colorado Springs to East Del Norte Street. The district also included Wahsatch Avenue from just north of downtown to East Columbia Street. Five blocks of Weber Street and two blocks of Wahsatch Avenue in the Old North End thus were located in this additional residential historic district.

The real goal of achieving National Register Historic District status for two portions of the Old North End was to change the attitude of residents of those two historic districts. It was intended to inspire those residents to think of their neighborhood as historically and architecturally significant and well worth preserving as close as possible to its original appearance.

An Active And Attractive Neighborhood

The Old North End is the only neighborhood in Colorado Springs to voluntarily develop its own master plan. The plan, which was approved by Colorado Springs City Council in February 1991, addresses seven major goals: improvements in transportation, public infrastructure, land use and zoning, parks and amenities, environment, neighborhood quality, and historic preservation.

In 2000, using guidelines developed by J. Mark Nelson and through the leadership of Pat Doyle, historic preservation overlay zoning was instituted in the historic core of the neighborhood. Another notable accomplishment was the 2007 installation of historic-style streetlights on North Tejon Street. Then, during the ONEN presidency of Dave Munger in 2009, heavy truck traffic was banned on North Nevada Avenue.

Neighborhood residents, under capable and talented leaders, continue to work hard to enhance and preserve the historic character of their lovely homes in the Old North End.

The Architecture of the Old North End

by Jennifer Wendler Lovell

Neighborhood Character

The Old North End neighborhood is recognized as the most intact collection of turn-of-the-century residential architecture in Colorado Springs. The neighborhood has great visual continuity due to its high concentration of well-maintained historic homes that employ high-quality materials, design, and craftsmanship. However, each house has its own distinctive character. There are over twenty architectural styles represented in the neighborhood and a great variety of house types, forms, and sizes. It is this architectural diversity that makes the Old North End neighborhood so unique.

It is not only the homes that give the Old North End its historic charm. The wide streets, mature shade trees, landscaped medians, and large, well-tended front yards all contribute considerably to the character of the neighborhood. Both the architecture and the setting work together to provide a tangible link to the past and give one the feeling of stepping back in time.

Cascade Avenue, c. 1916
(Photograph by Photo Craft Shop, courtesy Special Collections, Pikes Peak Library District. Image 001-5019.)

The Old North End neighborhood is easily navigable, as it is generally laid out in a grid pattern. Wide north/south streets, most with landscaped medians, are intersected by narrower east/west streets, creating rectangular blocks bisected by alleys. The western side of the neighborhood, near Monument Valley Park, deviates somewhat from the grid plan, as several of its streets curve to follow the contours of the park.

1222 N. Cascade Avenue, undated
(Courtesy Special Collections, Tutt Library, Colorado College, Colorado Springs, Colorado.)

House Types

Homes in the Old North End can be categorized into three house types: Mansions/Estates (two or two-and-one-half stories), Grand Homes (one-and-one-half to two-and-one half stories), and Cottages/Bungalows (one or one-and-one-half stories). A combination of these house types can be found throughout the neighborhood, but several areas have a greater concentration of one specific type. The southern blocks of the neighborhood along Wood and Cascade Avenues have houses that are predominantly Mansions/Estates and Grand Homes. Tejon Street and Nevada Avenue houses are primarily Grand Homes, and the majority of the houses north of Fontanero Street are Cottages/Bungalows. In general, larger houses are found on the wider north/south streets and smaller houses are found on the narrower east/west streets.

Neighborhood Development

Most homes in the Old North End neighborhood were constructed during the late 1800s and early 1900s. This period corresponded with great advances in building technology, including the mechanization of many

Architect rendering of 1325 N. Cascade Avenue, c. 1902
(Courtesy Special Collections, Pikes Peak Library District.)

construction tools and the mass production of building materials. The national railroad network made it possible to acquire a wide variety of structural and decorative manufactured building parts. Entire house kits, in which every piece necessary to build a house was shipped via railway, also became available in the early 20th century. In addition, house pattern books and trade periodicals were widely distributed and kept homeowners, builders, and architects informed of the fashionable architectural styles of the day.

Many of the neighborhood's homes were designed by well-known, influential architects, including Thomas MacLaren, Charles Thomas, Douglas & Hetherington, Frederick Sterner, E. C. G. Robinson, Barber & Hastings, Nicholas Van den Arend, and Frank Edbrook.

The neighborhood's earliest homes are largely concentrated in the southern areas of the neighborhood, but several early examples can be seen throughout the Old North End. In general, the northern portion of the neighborhood developed later and therefore displays architectural styles popular during the early 20th century. As the neighborhood grew, a number of homeowners sold off portions of their large lots for new construction, or previously unoccupied lots were built upon. This practice, known as infill construction, is the reason that houses of different architectural periods are often intermingled in the Old North End. This is especially evident in the western portion of the neighborhood near Monument Valley Park, where infill construction continued through the mid-20th century.

Architectural Features

Houses in the Old North End represent a wide variety of architectural styles, which are discussed in detail in the following chapter. However, a number of architectural features are common to many of the neighborhood's homes, regardless of style or size. The vast majority of Old North End homes are of wood frame construction and have wood shingle or wood clapboard siding. Most homes also have large front porches, decorative wood detailing, and masonry foundations. Other common features include irregular rooflines, dormers, elaborate front doorways, leaded or stained glass windows, and low wood or iron fences. Many houses were designed so that the southern or "sunny" side of the house contained the most frequently used living spaces, such as the living room, dining room and master bedroom. Bay windows are often located on the southern elevation for this reason. Another feature commonly seen in Old North End homes is the sleeping porch, which was often used by family members or boarders under treatment for tuberculosis. Although many sleeping porches were part of the original design of the house, some were later additions.

Most Old North End properties also contain one or more historic outbuildings. These include carriage houses, stables, garages, servant's quarters, and sheds. Several large historic outbuildings have since been converted to residences.

Children playing in the median at the 1600 block of N. Nevada Avenue, c. 1910
(Courtesy Special Collections, Pikes Peak Library District. Image 229-6008.)

Preservation

The Old North End retains a high degree of its original architectural integrity. This is due in large part to its homeowners and their commitment to preserving the historic character of the neighborhood. This includes the diligent maintenance of their historic homes, retaining historic materials and features when possible, replacing severely deteriorated materials and features in kind, and designing architecturally compatible additions when they are necessary.

Architectural Style Guide

Italianate

Popular from 1840 to 1885, the Italianate style was based on informal rural Italian residences. In the United States, the style was most common in the Midwest and Northeast, but examples can be seen throughout the country.

1705 N. Tejon Street

Typical features include:

- Two or three stories
- Square or rectangular plan
- Low-pitched roof with wide, bracketed eaves
- Tall, narrow windows, frequently arched or curved
- Elaborated window hoods
- Small, single-story porches with square supports

Queen Anne

The Queen Anne style was the most popular style of domestic architecture in the United States from 1880 through 1900. Although the style was named by a group of 19th century English architects, it was freely interpreted by American architects to include elaborations not seen in English precedents. Queen Anne houses are most easily identified by their irregular rooflines and varied wall surfaces. Many plans incorporate towers, turrets, bay windows and mixed siding materials. They also typically have partial, full-width or wrap-around porches. There are several subtypes of the Queen Anne style, based on their decorative detailing. Most of these subtypes are represented in the Old North End neighborhood:

Detail view of spindlework in gable

1339 N. Nevada Avenue

Spindlework: This Queen Anne subtype features delicate ornamentation, such as thin turned columns and spindlework, or gingerbread, woodwork. About 50 percent of Queen Anne houses in the United States are included in this subtype.

Free Classic/Edwardian:

The Free Classic subtype, also referred to as Edwardian style, became popular in the 1890s. It shares some features with early Colonial Revival style houses. Heavier classical columns and rails are used to support porches. Classical features such as

1601 N. Nevada Avenue

Palladian windows, cornice dentils, and pediments are also common. About 35 percent of Queen Anne houses in the United States represent the Free Classic subtype.

Half-Timbered:

The Half-Timbered subtype is more closely related to English precedents of the Queen Anne style. Decorative half-timbering is present in the gables or upper story walls. About 5 percent of Queen Anne houses in the United States are included in this subtype.

1520 N. Nevada Avenue

Eastlake

The Eastlake style is sometimes considered a type of ornamentation rather than a separate architectural style. The style is named for English architect Charles L. Eastlake, who wrote the book *Hints on Household Taste* in 1868. The book featured furniture designs that were more geometric and angular than the other elaborate styles of the day. American architects borrowed Eastlake's design principles and included oversized, angular decorative elements in their Victorian house plans.

114 W. Del Norte Street

Typical features include:

- Towers and irregular rooflines
- Heavy, angular ornamentation
- Massive turned porch supports

Detail view of Eastlake ornamentation

Shingle

The Shingle style, popular from 1880 to 1900, combines features seen in several other styles. Its asymmetrical forms and large porches are borrowed from the Queen Anne style. Palladian windows, classical columns, and gambrel roofs are adapted from Colonial examples, and wide arches and heavy stone bases are borrowed from the Richardson Romanesque style. The unifying feature of all Shingle style houses is the continuous wood shingle siding. The style has little decorative detailing and instead emphasizes a complex shape within a smooth surface.

1530 N. Cascade Avenue

Typical features include:
- Complex roofline with half towers and dormers
- Wood shingle siding without cornerboards
- Little decorative detailing around doors/windows
- Extensive porches with classical columns, square shingled columns, or stone piers

Gable End Frame

This house form is simply a frame house with the gable end turned toward the street. The design is particularly suited for narrow urban lots and was commonly used throughout the United States in the 19th and 20th centuries. Most Gable End Frame houses are minimally detailed, although some exhibit features of contemporaneous architectural styles such as Queen Anne or Colonial Revival.

17 W. Buena Ventura Street

Typical features include:

- Relatively steeply-pitched front-gabled roof
- Wood shingle or clapboard siding
- Simple details

Colonial Revival

The Colonial Revival style was the most popular domestic building style in the United States for the first half of the 20th century. The style flourished following the Philadelphia Centennial of 1876, which brought about a renewed interest in the colonial architectural traditions of the East Coast. Many examples of Colonial Revival houses freely combine details of the Georgian, Federal, and Dutch Colonial styles of that region.

1230 N. Cascade Avenue

Typical features include:

- Hip or side-gabled roof
- Gambrel roof (Dutch Colonial Revival)
- Cornices with modillions or dentils
- Classical columns
- Entry door with sidelights, fanlights or pediments
- Double-hung windows with multiple panes
- Palladian windows

Tudor/Elizabethan/Jacobean

The Tudor style is loosely based on several late Medieval English precedents. The earliest American houses in the style, built around the turn of the 19th century, were patterned after buildings from the Elizabethan or Jacobean eras of English history and are often considered a subtype of the Tudor style. In the 1920s and 1930s, the Tudor style became very fashionable in the United States and was rivaled in popularity only by the Colonial Revival style.

1332 N. Cascade Avenue

Typical features include:

- Steeply-pitched front gables which often overlap
- Decorative half-timbering
- Elaborate chimneys
- Patterned brickwork
- Leaded glass windows

French Eclectic

The French Eclectic style incorporates features from a broad period of French architecture. For that reason, the style shows great variety in detailing. The steeply-pitched roof, however, is a common feature of most French Eclectic residences. Although the style is relatively uncommon, it can be found throughout the United States.

1504 Alamo Avenue

Typical features include:

- Steeply-pitched hip roof
- Brick, stone, or stucco wall cladding
- Double-hung or casement windows
- Plank shutters

Neoclassical

Following the 1893 Columbian Exposition in Chicago, there was a renewed interest in classical architecture in the United States. The most well-known architects of the day designed buildings for the event in the mandated classical theme. The exposition was well attended and widely publicized, making the Neoclassical style fashionable throughout the country.

1308 N. Cascade Avenue

Typical features include:

- Hip or side-gabled roof
- Boxed eaves with modillions or dentils beneath
- Full-height porch, usually with a classical pediment
- Massive classical columns
- Symmetrical façade

Italian Renaissance Revival

Unlike earlier Italianate style houses, which were loose interpretations of informal Italian farmhouses, Italian Renaissance Revival houses were directly modeled after the grand Renaissance residences of Italy. Popular from 1890 to 1935, the style was less common than the contemporaneous Colonial Revival, Tudor, and Craftsman styles. Prior to World War I, the style was primarily used for architect designed landmark houses.

1228 Wood Avenue

Typical features include:
- Low-pitched hip roof, usually tiled
- Wide eaves with brackets
- Stucco or masonry walls
- Arched doors and windows
- Arcaded porches
- Smaller, less elaborate upper story windows

Spanish Mission

Popular between 1890 and 1920, the Spanish Mission style is an adaptation of Spanish Colonial Mission buildings. The style gained recognition after 1893 when it was used for the California Building at the Columbian Exposition in Chicago. The style was common in the Southwest, but scattered examples can be seen in early 20th century neighborhoods throughout the United States.

206 W. Del Norte Street

Typical features include:
- Tile roof with wide eaves
- Curvilinear parapet
- Stucco walls
- Arcaded porch, usually supported by large square piers
- Arched windows and/or doors

Spanish Colonial Revival

This style was popular from 1915 to 1940 and is most commonly seen in the southwestern states and Florida. Unlike the Spanish Mission style, the Spanish Colonial Revival style is inspired by the entire history of Spanish architecture. Decorative features may be borrowed from Moorish, Byzantine or Renaissance precedents.

1625 Culebra Place

Typical features include:

- Low-pitched tile roofs with little or no overhang
- Stucco wall surface
- Circular chimney
- Arched doors or windows
- Decorative ironwork on windows
- Arcaded wing wall

Prairie

The Prairie style originated in Chicago and is one of the few architectural styles that is indigenous to the United States. Frank Lloyd Wright and his followers, known as the Prairie School, believed that a building should be harmonious with its landscape. To that end, Prairie houses usually had a strong horizontal emphasis, which complemented the flat topography of the Midwest. A common subtype of the style, known as the Prairie Box or American Foursquare, features a square or rectangular plan and a hip roof.

1829 N. Nevada Avenue

Typical features include:
- Low-pitched hip roof
- Hip dormers
- Wide, boxed eaves
- Built-in planter boxes
- Square piers supporting porch

Craftsman

The Craftsman style was greatly influenced by the English Arts and Crafts movement and its rejection of the Industrial Revolution. Another influence on the Craftsman style was the exotic architecture of the Orient. Although a number of large landmark examples of the Craftsman style exist, especially in California, the most popular expression of the style is the Craftsman bungalow. Through pattern books and popular magazines, the Craftsman bungalow became the most fashionable small house in the country in the early 20th century.

1331 N. Wahsatch Avenue

Typical features include:

- Low-pitched hip or gable roof
- Wide eaves with exposed rafter tails or brackets
- Large porches with square or battered columns
- Double-hung windows with multi-paned upper sash

Bungalow/Cottage

The terms "bungalow" or "cottage" describe a smaller house of simple design. Although they may exhibit some features of a particular style, they are smaller in scale and less formal in design. In the Old North End neighborhood, a number of bungalows and cottages were designed with Queen Anne, Georgian, and Tudor features. Some are designed without an attempt to mimic a particular style and are often described as "vernacular."

1220 N. Wahsatch Avenue

Typical features include:

- One to one-and-one-half stories in height
- Simple, compact plan
- Large porch
- May exhibit features of various contemporaneous styles

International Style

In 1932, a groundbreaking show at the Museum of Modern Art in New York called "Modern Architecture: International Exhibition" exposed Americans to the radically different buildings being designed by European architects. The International style, as it came to be known, was based on a rejection of historical stylistic references. Functionalism was emphasized, and purely decorative features were considered superfluous.

205 W. Fontanero Street

Typical features include:

- Flat roof
- Horizontal emphasis
- Geometric simplicity
- Large expanses of glass
- Unadorned wall surface
- Windows flush with walls

Monument Valley
Park Area Tour

□ Featured Property
→ Tour Route

N

Tour 1
Monument Valley Park Area

1400 Block of Alamo Avenue, looking south, 2010

Begin the tour at 1414 Culebra Avenue, just north of W. Columbia Street. The tour ends at 115 W. Columbia Street, just west of Wood Avenue. The distance of the tour is approximately 1.5 miles.

1414 Culebra Avenue

Harry Jackson, long-time president of the Y.M.C.A., built this house in 1909 for his daughter Sara and her husband Dr. Phillip Loomis. Dr. Loomis was a physician and a nationally known iris hybridizer. For many years, the home's gardens were opened to the public for one week in June when the irises were

1414 Culebra Avenue

in bloom. The house is Shingle style with some Tudor influences. It has wood shingle siding, a varied roofline, and stone porches and chimneys.

1535 Culebra Avenue

This Cape Cod style house was built in 1933 by Jane Quackenbush Bennett. In 1936, she married Joseph J. Dern, a director and officer of the First Federal Savings and Loan Association. He was also the president of the Dern Company, a coffee shop formerly located on Tejon Street known for its "Derngood" coffee.

1535 Culebra Avenue

Typical of the Cape Cod style, the house has a steeply pitched gable roof with small gable dormers and multi-paned double-hung windows with shutters.

1614 Culebra Place

The arched wall dormers and small oculus window adjacent to the front door are unique features of this Colonial Revival style house. It was built in 1948 by contractor C. A. Carlson for owners William and Gladys Nicoll. Mr. Nicoll was president of the Nicoll Warehouse Company.

1614 Culebra Place

1625 Culebra Place

Designed in the Spanish Colonial Revival style, this home was built in 1937 by Albert and Fern Cooper. Mr. Cooper was the chief engineer at the Holly Sugar Company. The house was constructed by builder A. J. Betty. Interesting architectural features include the red tile roof, circular chimney, and arcaded wing wall.

1625 Culebra Place

314 W. Del Norte Street

Architect Thomas MacLaren designed this Prairie style house in 1912. The half-timbering in the gables displays some secondary Tudor influence. The home was built for George K. Shields, secretary-treasurer of Van Briggle Pottery, and his wife Edna. Later owners included Dr. George Bancroft, former chief of staff at

314 W. Del Norte Street

St. Francis and Memorial hospitals, and O. Donald Olson, former president of the Exchange National Bank.

220 W. Del Norte Street

Built in 1936, this Tudor style house features multiple front gables and decorative half-timbering in the second story. The home's first owners were Ben and Mary Wendelken. Mr. Wendelken was a long-time trial attorney and served as Colorado Springs city attorney from 1931 to 1947.

220 W. Del Norte Street

1725 Culebra Place

Contractor Otto Engleking built this Spanish Colonial Revival style house in 1929 for Mrs. Lydia E. Leslie. It was later owned by Robin P. Aldridge, president of the Aldridge Mercantile Company. Prominent features of the house include the red tile roof, the cantilevered balcony, and the massive front chimney.

1725 Culebra Place

1801 Culebra Avenue

This Spanish Colonial Revival style house was designed by architect Thomas MacLaren in 1911. (See call-out, next page.) The house is rectangular in plan with a tile roof, exposed rafter tails, stucco walls, and an arched door surround featuring a decorative medallion. It was built for Dr. Henry C. Watt and his

1801 Culebra Avenue

wife Marjorie. Dr. Watt was the personal physician of General William Jackson Palmer, founder of Colorado Springs. Marjorie Watt was Palmer's daughter. She was a well-known philanthropist. In 1922, she created a nutrition camp

1801 Culebra Avenue soon after its construction
(Photograph by Photo Craft Shop, courtesy Special Collections, Pikes Peak Library District. Image 044-9031.)

for malnourished children at her home. The camp was later moved to Glockner Sanitorium (now Penrose Hospital). Dr. Henry Watt died in 1917. When Marjorie Watt's health required her to move to England in 1923, she donated her home, all of its furnishings, and $110,000 to the Sunnyrest Sanatorium, a tuberculosis treatment facility in Colorado Springs.

Architect Thomas MacLaren

Born in Perthshire, Scotland, in 1863, Thomas MacLaren came to Colorado in 1892 to seek a cure for his tuberculosis. He was a talented young architect who had been trained at the Royal Academy of Arts in London and had won numerous awards for his architectural drawings.

(Courtesy Special Collections, Tutt Library, Colorado College, Colorado Springs, Colorado.)

He moved to Colorado Springs in 1894 and established a prosperous business, first as an independent architect and later in partnerships with architects C. E. Thomas and T. D. Hetherington. During his 34 years of practice in Colorado Springs, he designed more than two hundred buildings. MacLaren worked in a broad range of architectural styles and advocated strongly for architectural designs that complemented the landscape of the region. He was highly respected and was credited with contributing greatly to the artistic atmosphere of the city. He designed such prominent public buildings as St. Stephens Episcopal Church, Colorado Springs City Hall, Fire Station No. 1, the City Auditorium, the clubhouse at Patty Jewett Golf Course, and the original Steele School.

Thomas MacLaren's residential designs were also highly regarded and were featured in many architectural journals of the day. His most well-known domestic design was Claremont, an elaborate Broadmoor residence patterned after the Grand Trianon at Versailles. Many impressive examples of his residential work can be seen in the Old North End neighborhood, a number of which are featured in walking tours 1, 2, 3, 5, and 6.

205 W. Fontanero Street

Dr. Maurice Snyder, a pediatrician, and his wife Jane built this International style house in 1947. It was designed by architect Jan Ruhtenberg, a nationally known architect credited with making significant contributions to modern architecture in the United States. He was involved in the Bauhaus movement and

205 W. Fontanero Street

studied under Mies van der Rohe in Germany. The design of this house stresses horizontality with its flat roof and wide projecting eaves. Geometric simplicity is emphasized in its unadorned walls with windows mounted flush with the wall surface.

1918 El Parque Street

This sprawling estate house was built in 1917 by William and Constance Elmslie. Mrs. Elmslie was the youngest daughter of newspaper titan Joseph Pulitzer. She came to Colorado Springs in 1909 to be treated for tuberculosis by Dr. Gerald Webb. William Elmslie had been her brother's tutor and one of her

1918 El Parque Street

father's secretaries. He was later the secretary-treasurer of the Broadmoor Polo Association. The house features an irregular plan with a varied roofline and stucco walls. The property once had extensive gardens with red stone walls and lily ponds. The home has since been converted to multiple apartment units.

1903 El Parque Street

Fred and Adele Simpson built this Colonial Revival style house in 1942. Mr. Simpson was the president of the Simpson Grain Company, the Midland Bean Company, and the Colorado Title and Abstract Company. He also served as a Colorado Springs city council member from 1953 to 1959 and was mayor of the city from 1957 to 1959.

1903 El Parque Street

1821 Alamo Avenue

This unique house was originally built as a stable for the house located at 1830 Wood Ave. It was designed by architects MacLaren and Thomas for homeowner Berne Hopkins in 1914. It was later converted to a residence and was the long-time home of Norma W. Dodge, widow of Stuart P. Dodge. She was employed as an administrator of the Colorado Springs chapter of the American Red Cross for many years.

1821 Alamo Avenue

This c. 1914 photograph shows the Hopkins stable shortly after construction. Despite being converted to a residence, the exterior of the building has remained relatively unchanged. (Courtesy Special Collections, Pikes Peak Library District. Image 044-9547.)

206 W. Del Norte Street

Contractor Merle H. Timmons built this elegant house for physician William P. McCrossin and his wife Leonora in 1926. Designed in the Spanish Mission style, it features a tile roof with a curvilinear parapet and an arcaded entry porch.

206 W. Del Norte Street

211 W. Del Norte Street

Architect Edward Bunts designed this Cape Cod style house as his own residence in 1937. Other Bunts designs in Colorado Springs include the First Christian Church, the Masonic Temple, Palmer High School, the First United Methodist Church, and the El Paso County Judicial Building.

211 W. Del Norte Street

1617 Alamo Avenue

Built in 1922, this Spanish Mission style house was the longtime residence of Miss Chastine Olson. The design features an arcaded wing wall, arched windows, and a curvilinear parapet. The attached garage was a later addition.

1617 Alamo Avenue

126 W. Caramillo Street

Architect Charles Thomas designed this Spanish Mission style residence in 1923. The tile roof, shaped parapet, and arched windows are all typical of the style. The home's first occupants were Joseph and Irene Arnold. In 1930, it became the long-time residence of Charles and Josephine Orton. Mr. Orton was an attorney with the firm of Root & Orton.

126 W. Caramillo Street

126 W. Caramillo Street, c. 1923
(Courtesy Special Collections, Pikes Peak Library District. Image 001-9028.)

1505 Alamo Avenue

Designed in the Spanish Colonial Revival style, this residence was built by contractor C. A. Carlson in 1938. The house features an elaborate chimney top, red tile roof, and a small wrought iron balconettte. The first owner of the home was Mrs. Daisy Aley, widow of Hamilton W. Aley, who owned the Aley Drug Company.

1505 Alamo Avenue

1504 Alamo Avenue

This unique residence was built in 1930 by Roy and Ruth Foard. Roy Foard was an attorney in business with his two brothers at the Foard Brothers law firm. The house was designed in the French Eclectic style and has a steeply-pitched hip roof, plank shutters, and casement windows.

1504 Alamo Avenue

1433 Alamo Avenue

This three-story stucco house was built in 1924 by Mrs. F. W. Searby. It has several Tudor style features, including the elaborate chimneys and multiple gables. In 1936, it became the long-time home of physician Harry C. Goodson and his wife Alice.

1433 Alamo Avenue

1428 Alamo Avenue

Contractor C. A. Carlson built this Spanish Colonial Revival house for Ernest Florio, a salesman at the Boston Department Store in downtown Colorado Springs. Built in 1941, the design features stucco walls, a red tile roof, and a segmental arched entryway.

1428 Alamo Avenue

1428 Alamo Avenue, c. 1941

1406 Alamo Avenue

This Tudor style house was built in 1936 by contractor L. D. Shotwell for William L. Hazlett and his wife Helen. Mr. Hazlett was vice president of the Colorado Savings Bank of Colorado Springs. In 1940, the house became the residence of Floyd L. Kelsey, president of the Boston Department Store. The

1406 Alamo Avenue

design includes multiple front gables with patterned brickwork and decorative vergeboards.

115 W. Columbia Street

Architect Elizabeth Wright Ingraham, granddaughter of Frank Lloyd Wright, designed this modern house in 1951. It was built for urologist Robert Beadles and his wife Mildred, a schoolteacher. The home is minimally detailed, with a flat roof, wide overhanging eaves, and wide plank siding.

115 W. Columbia Street

Tour 2
Wood Avenue

1300 block of Wood Avenue, c. 1900
(Courtesy Special Collections, Pikes Peak Library District.)

Begin the tour at the northwest corner of Wood Avenue and Uintah Street. The tour ends at the northeast corner of Wood Avenue and Uintah Street. The distance of the tour is approximately 1.5 miles.

1206 Wood Avenue

Sherwood Aldrich, a banker, built this Shingle style house in 1901. In 1917, Cassius A. Hibbard, owner of Hibbard and Company department store, purchased the house. Hibbard's store was located on S. Tejon Street and opened in 1893. It was run by four generations of family members

1206 Wood Avenue

1206 Wood Avenue, c. 1901
(Photograph by F. P. Stevens and A. J. Harlan, courtesy Special Collections, Pikes Peak Library District. Image 257-6418.)

before closing in 1997. The home was designed by architect Frederick J. Sterner, who also designed General Palmer's residence, Glen Eyrie. Features of the house include the continuously shingled walls, large gable dormers, and massive stone piers supporting a gabled porch.

1210 Wood Avenue

This Colonial Revival style house was built by prominent attorney William O'Brien in 1899. He was also the principal stockholder in the Mollie Gibson Mining Company. The O'Brien family lived in the home until 1925. It was acquired by Colorado College from the Hendee family in 1955 and was formerly used

1210 Wood Avenue

as the home of the college's president. Designed by architects Douglas & Hetherington, the house features a semi-circular portico, a modillioned cornice, and projecting quoins at the corners.

This c. 1899 view of 1210 Wood Avenue shows the house under construction The hip roof porch and the original dormers have since been removed.
(Courtesy Special Collections, Pikes Peak Library District.)

1228 Wood Avenue

Denver architects Varian & Sterner designed this Italian Renaissance Revival style house for attorney R. J. Preston and his wife Elizabeth in 1898. Philip B. and Sarah F. Stewart purchased the house in 1902. Mr. Stewart was an attorney who was prominent in banking, utilities, and mining. He served as speaker

1228 Wood Avenue

of the state House of Representatives and chairman of the Republican Party. He was also a friend of Theodore Roosevelt, who stayed at the house during his presidency. Philip B. Stewart was a Colorado College trustee for over fifty years, and his home was bequeathed to the college upon his death in 1957. It now serves as the home of the president of Colorado College. The design features small wings at either end of the façade, which create a recess for an arcaded loggia. A similarly arcaded porch is located at the south side of the house. The pediments and balconettes on the second story windows and the raised quoins at the corners are also typical features of the Italian Renaissance Revival style.

1228 Wood Avenue, c. 1898
(Courtesy Special Collections, Pikes Peak Library District.)

1238 Wood Avenue

This 1905 house was built for Frederick and Alice Bemis Taylor. Mrs. Taylor was the daughter of manufacturing millionaire Judson Bemis and inherited his fortune after his death in 1921. She was a well-known philanthropist who financially supported numerous Colorado Springs institutions. (See call-out, next page.)

1238 Wood Avenue

Architect Charley K. Cummings of Boston designed the Tudor style house. It has a steeply-pitched roof with flared gables, gable wall dormers, and decorative half-timbering in the second story.

This undated photo of 1238 Wood Avenue shows that the front porch was once open and the half-timbering only decorated the rear portion of the house. (Courtesy Special Collections, Pikes Peak Library District. Image 001-1962.)

Alice Bemis Taylor

When longtime Old North End resident Alice Bemis Taylor died in 1942, the Colorado Springs Gazette described her as "Colorado Springs' Lady Bountiful." Indeed, she was best known as a civic-minded philanthropist and a selfless humanitarian.

Alice Bemis Taylor was born in Newton, Massachusetts, in 1877. Her father, Judson Bemis, was the founder of the world's largest manufacturer of

(Courtesy Special Collections, Pikes Peak Library District. Image 001-361.)

cloth and paper bags. The Bemis family moved to Colorado Springs in 1881, making their home at 506 N. Cascade Avenue.

Alice was married in 1903 to Frederick Pike Taylor, a nephew of the president of Vassar College. The couple built their home at 1238 Wood Avenue shortly thereafter.

A professed lover of architecture, Alice utilized her family fortune to construct several notable Colorado Springs buildings. She funded a new building for the Colorado Springs Day Nursery in 1923 and financed the construction of the Colorado Springs Fine Arts Center in 1936. Upon completion of the Fine Arts Center, she donated her extensive collection of southwestern art and artifacts to the museum.

In 1934, Alice Bemis Taylor became the first woman to serve on the Colorado College Board of Trustees. Taylor Hall at the college was later named in her honor. Upon her death, the majority of her fortune was left to the Fine Arts Center, the Day Nursery, and Colorado College.

1306 Wood Avenue

1306 Wood Avenue

The W. R. Roby Lumber Company built this striking house for Mrs. Milnora Roberts in 1891 at a cost of $14,000. In 1895, James J. Hagerman, owner of the Colorado Midland Railway Company, purchased the house for Percy Hagerman, his son. Percy Hagerman was the president of the Mollie Gibson Consolidated Mining & Milling Company and was an avid outdoorsman and mountaineer. Hagerman Peak, near Aspen, is named in his honor. The three-story Shingle style house has a stone base, wood shingled walls, and a steeply-pitched side-gabled roof. Interesting details include the Palladian windows on the north and south elevations, an eyebrow dormer on the façade, and massive stone pillars supporting the engaged front porch.

William W. Hassell

As president of the Hassell Iron Works Company, Old North End resident William W. Hassell was responsible for the creation of many of the early iron fences in Colorado Springs.

Mr. Hassell came to Colorado Springs in 1885 seeking a cure for his tuberculosis. After his health improved, he purchased a foot-powered machine used for weaving wood pickets with wire to make fencing. He soon branched out into light iron work and electrical supplies.

(Courtesy Special Collections, Tutt Library, Colorado College, Colorado Springs, Colorado.)

After his first two shops were destroyed in two separate fires, a new foundry was established on Sierra Madre Street adjoining the Midland Railroad tracks. The company dropped the electrical supply business and focused on the production of iron and brass castings, machinery, and structural and ornamental iron work. At its peak during World War I, Hassell Iron Works employed 125 people.

Following William W. Hassell's death in 1922, his son W. Bradford Hassell took over management of the iron works. He and his sister, Julia Hassell Lipsey, eventually sold the company in 1938.

Hassell Iron Works is perhaps best known for the numerous ornamental fences that still border the properties of historic Colorado Springs homes today. Examples of Hassell Iron Works fences in the Old North End are noted in the walking tours with a fleur-de-lis symbol ⚜, which was a common Hassell fence motif.

1424 Wood Avenue

This c. 1895 house was the long-time residence of William W. Hassell and his family. Mr. Hassell was the president of Hassell Iron Works, manufacturer of the ornamental fencing that borders many homes in the Old North End and other historic neighborhoods in Colorado Springs. (See call-out, previous

1424 Wood Avenue

page.) The photograph below shows that the house has been altered significantly since its construction. It was originally a Gable End Frame house with wood clapboard siding. It has since had several additions to the south elevation and has been clad in stucco. The porch has been replaced, and a balcony has been added above the new porch. ⚜

1424 Wood Avenue, c. 1900
(Courtesy Special Collections, Pikes Peak Library District. Image 001-9535.)

1432 Wood Avenue

The cross-gambrel roof, leaded glass Palladian window, and full-width porch are distinctive features of this Dutch Colonial Revival house. It was built c. 1896 and was for many years the home of David N. Heizer and his family. He was a Cripple Creek mining investor and a director of Colorado Springs

1432 Wood Avenue

National Bank. He also served as mayor of Colorado Springs from 1906 to 1908. During his term, he initiated Pike's Peak Northslope water development, paved city sidewalks, and completed Monument Valley Park. The Heizer family owned the residence until 1945.

1520 Wood Avenue

Architect Thomas MacLaren designed this residence for Charles P. Bennett, president of Bennett-Schellenberger Realty. The house was built in 1901 and has many elements of the Shingle style, including its continuous wood shingle wall cladding, two-story bay window, and shed dormers. The large overhanging front gable has a recessed grouping of four windows, which is also typical of the style. Other prominent features of the façade include the large wrap-around porch and the full-width balcony.

1520 Wood Avenue

Architect Thomas MacLaren's c. 1901 rendering of 1520 Wood Avenue.
(Courtesy Special Collections, Pikes Peak Library District.)

1528 Wood Avenue

Children's book author Sidford Hamp built this Gable End Frame residence in 1906. His wife Josephine was the daughter of R. R. Cable, who was president of the Rock Island Railroad. The house has wood shingle siding, large two-story bay windows, and an overhanging third story gable supported by brackets. ❖

1528 Wood Avenue

1604 Wood Avenue

This Thomas MacLaren-designed residence shares many of the stylistic elements of the house at 1520 Wood Avenue, including the wood shingle siding, the overhung bracketed second story, the shed dormer, and the recessed gable windows. The house was built in 1904 for William W. Postlethwaite, who was General

1604 Wood Avenue

William Jackson Palmer's personal secretary. After Palmer's death, Postlethwaite served as treasurer of Colorado College and later as curator of the college museum.

114 W. Del Norte Street

Rose M. Durkee, who also built the house at 1700 Wood, built this Eastlake style house in 1903. The earliest residents were dentist William S. Twilley and his wife Cora. It was later the long-time home of W. D. Corley, builder of Corley Mountain Highway, now known as Gold Camp Road. Corley operated the scenic

114 W. Del Norte Street

highway as a toll road from 1924 to 1939. Typical of the Eastlake style, the house has heavy, angular decorative elements, including the large eave brackets and decorative woodwork in the gables. The roofline is varied, with clipped cross-gables and a small octagonal tower. The façade features a full-width enclosed porch with a balcony above and a large bowed window on the second story.

1700 Wood Avenue

Architects Douglas & Hetherington designed this charming Queen Anne style house in 1903. It was built by contractor William A. Guzman for Rose M. Durkee. She was the widow of merchant Charles E. Durkee and the daughter of D. Russ Wood, namesake of Wood Avenue. The house has a hip roof

1700 Wood Avenue

with two lower cross-gables and a uniquely squat round tower. The first story and tower have wood clapboard siding, and the gables have wood shingle siding.

1738 Wood Avenue

Robert P. Davie and his wife Martha built this grand residence in 1906. Mr. Davie was president of the Davie Realty Company and the Davie Building & Investment Company. A later long-term owner was Courtland V. Edgar, president of the Arkansas-Vancouver Timber and Lumber Company. The house is

1738 Wood Avenue

rectangular in plan with a hip roof. The design exhibits a decidedly Craftsman influence in its low-pitched gabled front porch and wide eaves with exposed rafter tails.

1806 Wood Avenue

Construction on this Colonial Revival style residence began in 1902. Just as it was nearing completion in January 1903, a fire completely destroyed the house. The owner, Dr. Alfred A. Blackman, decided to rebuild the house almost immediately using the original plan. Dr. Blackman began his career as a surgeon

1806 Wood Avenue

but later became a psychotherapist. He served as medical advisor at Colorado College and was a member of the staff at Beth-El Hospital. The house has a hip roof with a large front-gabled dormer. The façade also features a partial-width front porch and a front door with an elliptical fanlight and sidelights. The shed-roofed projection on the south elevation is a later addition.

1830 Wood Avenue

Architect Thomas MacLaren designed this Tudor style residence in 1906 for owner Thomas Curtin. He was the president of the Grand Junction and Grand River Valley Falls Railway Company. In 1914, the home was purchased by petroleum and mining entrepreneur Berne Hopkins, who added a music

1830 Wood Avenue

room, greenhouse, stable and garage. J. Don Alexander purchased the house in 1930. He was president of the Alexander Film Company, which produced commercials and trailers for motion pictures. He was also the president of Alexander Aircraft, known for producing the first plane with retractable landing gear. The house was designed with brick walls on the first story, stucco on the second and third stories, and decorative half-timbering in the gables.

1815 Wood Avenue

This bungalow exhibits classical detailing in its paired fluted columns, corner pilasters, and gabled front porch. The second story gable is a later addition. The house was built in 1909 by James J. Waring. He was a young medical student when he came to Colorado Springs for tuberculosis treatment, and he lived here with

1815 Wood Avenue

his mother and aunt during his convalescence. The family moved to Denver in 1911 so that James could resume his medical studies. He was later appointed Professor of Medicine and head of the Department of Medicine at the University of Colorado. After the death of local tuberculosis specialist Dr. Gerald Webb, the Webb Institute for Medical Research moved from Colorado Springs to Denver. Dr. Waring became president of the Institute. When he died in 1962, the institute was renamed the Webb-Waring Institute for Biomedical Research.

1729 Wood Avenue

This cross-gambrel roofed house was built c. 1902. Its earliest residents were Alex Smith, president of the Star and Crescent Creamery, and his wife Amanda. By 1911, Justus R. Friedline occupied the home. He was president of the Russell Produce Company. Stuart Dodge, a reporter at the *Colorado Springs*

1729 Wood Avenue

Gazette, and his wife Norma were later residents. The house exhibits features of both the Dutch Colonial Revival and Shingle styles. It has continuous wood shingle siding, a prominent front cross-gambrel, and a wrap-around porch supported by classical columns.

1629 Wood Avenue

This Queen Anne style house was built in 1902 for physician Pliny Perkins. It has a cross-gabled roof, wood shingle siding, a shed wall dormer, and turreted porches decorated with spindlework.

1629 Wood Avenue

20 W. Caramillo Street

Sisters Sarah and Ella Warren built this Colonial Revival style house in 1902. Ella Warren died in 1903, just after the house was completed. Sarah Warren was one of the founders of the Day Nursery and served as president of the board. Their brother, Edward Warren, boarded at the house for many years. He was a nationally

20 W. Caramillo Street

known naturalist, authoring several books on the wildlife of Colorado. He was also director of the Colorado College Museum. The home remained in the Warren family until 1973. Designed by architects Douglas & Hetherington and constructed by builders Honeyman & Auld, the house has wood shingle siding, a bay window, and a partial-width front porch and balcony.

1531 Wood Avenue

Another Thomas MacLaren design, this Dutch Colonial Revival style home was built for eastern businessman E. E. Dunwoody in 1900. The design features a cross-gambrel roof, wood clapboard siding, and a full-width porch and balcony. A two-story bay window on the south elevation and a small oriel window on the north elevation complete the composition.

1531 Wood Avenue

1501 Wood Avenue

The first residents of this c.1897 Shingle style residence were Rev. William Fish and his wife Helen. Rev. Fish was the pastor at All Souls Unitarian Church. Later owners included: Rev. William W. Ranney, pastor of the First Congregational Church; Asa W. Parker, one of the leading amateur chess players in the country; and Dennis O'Rourke, president of the Holly Sugar Company. The massive front facing gambrel is the dominant feature of this unique house. The second and third stories of the house are clad in wood shingles, while the first story has wood clapboard siding. The wide front porch and balcony are recent additions, and the once open-air porches on the east and west elevations have since been enclosed.

1501 Wood Avenue

1501 Wood Avenue can been seen in the background of this c. 1899 photograph. It was taken during the city's annual flower carnival, when residents decorated their carriages and drove them around the city. (Courtesy Denver Public Library, Western History Collection, James B. Brown, X-18226.)

18 W. Buena Ventura Street

Cassius R. Manning and his wife Kizzie built this Colonial Revival style house in c. 1897. Mr. Manning was one of the city's leading attorneys and went on to serve as police magistrate for many years. The symmetrical design of the house features a hip roof with a gable dormer, a small

18 W. Buena Ventura Street

balcony, and a full-width porch supported by classical columns. The unique glazing pattern in the upper sash of the double-hung windows is a highlight of the façade.

Another c. 1899 photograph from the flower carnival shows 18 W. Buena Ventura Street in the background. The decorative balustrade on the third story dormer has since been removed. (Courtesy Denver Public Library, Western History Collection, James B. Brown, X-18247.)

17 W. Buena Ventura Street

This two-story Gable End Frame house was built c. 1902. It was the long-time home of David V. Donaldson and his wife Anne. Mr. Donaldson was the first manager of the Colorado Springs park system, founder of the Mining Exchange, and trustee for the gift of the Garden of the

17 W. Buena Ventura Street

Gods Park to the city. He was also a founder of the Broadmoor Art Academy.

1409 Wood Avenue

This unique Shingle style house was built c. 1899 and features a circular tower and an octagonal dormer. In 1920, it became the long-time home of W. Francis Hamp, his wife Linda, and their daughter Julia. Julia Hamp continued to live in the house until her death in 1977. She was active in the Girl Scouts for over

1409 Wood Avenue

60 years, serving as president of the local Girl Scout Council three times. She was elected to the National Girl Scout Board in 1955 and was the first woman to receive the Colorado Senior League Service Award in 1972.

1329 Wood Avenue

This fine example of the Shingle style was designed by architects Douglas & Hetherington in 1897. It has a stone foundation and front porch, wood shingled walls, and a gambrel roof. The large cross-gable on the façade features a unique bowed window and several casement windows. The house was built for Eugene

1329 Wood Avenue

P. Shove, part owner of Shove-Hager & Company, which dealt in investment securities. He was also on the Board of Trustees of Colorado College and donated Shove Memorial Chapel to the college. The home was later the residence of Andrew Marshall, former city council member and mayor of Colorado Springs from 1973 to 1975.

1329 Wood Avenue, c. 1897
(Courtesy Special Collections, Pikes Peak Library District.)

1321 Wood Avenue

Architect Frederick J. Sterner designed this Colonial Revival style house in 1897. It was built for Frederick H. Morley, who was secretary and treasurer of the Shields-Morley Grocery Company, vice president of the Colorado Springs Gas & Electric Company, and president of the First National Bank of Colorado

1321 Wood Avenue

Springs. The two-story, hip roof house has a stone foundation, wood shingled walls, and an arcaded front porch with paired columns. The façade features a large arched window and a small balcony on the second story.

1321 Wood Avenue, c. 1897
(Courtesy Special Collections, Pikes
Peak Library District.)

1315 Wood Avenue

1315 Wood Avenue

Architects Douglas & Hetherington designed this Dutch Colonial Revival style house in 1897. It was built for Nelson B. Williams, president of the Isabella Mining Company, at a cost of $15,000. In 1902, the house was purchased by mining investor James F. Burns. He was part owner of the Portland Mine, which became the single richest gold mine in the Cripple Creek Mining District. (See call-out, next page.) When built, the house was three stories with a gambrel roof and a prominent two-story cross-gambrel with a Palladian window. In 1909, Mr. Burns hired the original architects to design a large addition to the southern end of the house that included a second cross-gambrel on the façade. The home's large flat-roofed porch with paired columns was also expanded. Once completed, the house was considered the showplace of Millionaire's Row on Wood Avenue. The Burns family owned the house until 1940. It has since been converted into multiple apartment units.

This historic photograph shows the Williams-Burns house prior to the 1909 addition. (Courtesy Special Collections, Pikes Peak Library District.)

James F. Burns

Mining millionaire James "Jimmie" Burns was born in Portland, Maine, on January 8, 1853. He came to Colorado Springs at the age of 33 with his sisters and a teenaged orphan named James Doyle.

Reports of rich gold strikes attracted Burns to Cripple Creek, Colorado. In 1891, he and James Doyle staked a small claim on Battle Mountain. They named the claim Portland, for their hometown. Upon the

JAMES F. BURNS.

(Courtesy Special Collections, Pikes Peak Library District. Image 001-8637.)

discovery of large amounts of gold, they soon formed the Portland Gold Mining Company with the help of another partner, John Harmon. Burns was put in charge of Portland's operations and remained the company's president until he resigned in 1905. The Portland Mine became known as the "Queen of Cripple Creek" and made James Burns a multi-millionaire.

Burns married Miss Octavia Bell Parker in 1901. The couple purchased the grand house at 1315 Wood Avenue shortly thereafter. They had two children, James F. Burns, Jr., and Gladys Helen Burns.

Aside from his mining interests, James Burns was also a director of the First National Bank of Colorado Springs and the owner of the now demolished Burns Theater. Formerly located near the corner of Cascade and Pikes Peak Avenues, the ornate theater was known as the finest show house in the West. James Burns died in 1917 at the age of 54. His beloved theater was renamed the Chief Theater in 1933 and was torn down in 1973.

1215 Wood Avenue

Architects Douglas & Hetherington designed this home for Mr. Douglas' relatives Abbie T. and Sarah M. Lansing. Abbie T. Lansing later married E. L. Kernochan of the Stokes-Kernochan Insurance Agency, and the couple made their home in the house. Later residents were the Gilpin family. Frank

1215 Wood Avenue

Gilpin was a furniture maker and broker. His daughter, Laura Gilpin, was an internationally known photographer who published four books of photography on the American southwest. The house exhibits a number of Craftsman style features, including its wide, bracketed eaves and exposed rafter tails in the hip dormers and shed roof projection.

1215 Wood Avenue can be seen under construction at left in this c. 1909 photograph. (Courtesy of Special Collections, Tutt Library, Colorado College, Colorado Springs, Colorado.)

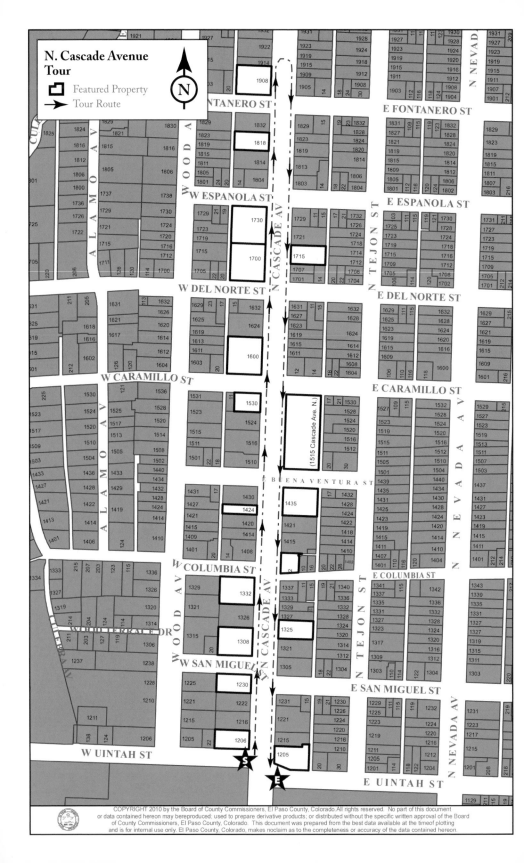

Tour 3
N. Cascade Avenue

1300 block of N. Cascade Avenue, looking north, c. 1910
(Courtesy Colorado Historical Society, Image CHS.X5334.)

Begin the tour at the northwest corner of N. Cascade Avenue and Uintah Street. The tour ends at the northeast corner of N. Cascade and Uintah Street. The distance of the tour is approximately 1.5 miles.

1206 N. Cascade Avenue

Reverend C. C. Dickey, a former Presbyterian minister and real estate investor, built this house in 1890. It was designed by architects Barber and Hastings and cost $18,000 to construct. The home was listed in the *Colorado Springs Gazette* as one of the most expensive residences built in Colorado Springs that year. It

1206 N. Cascade Avenue

was later purchased by C. B. Seldomridge, part owner of Seldomridge Bros., a wholesale flour, grain, and hay business. Although the house has been altered considerably since construction, it once exhibited elements of both the Shingle and Elizabethan styles. As seen in the historic photo at left, the house once

had wood shingle siding on the second story and decorative half-timbering in the gables. The large two-story gabled portion on the west elevation is also a later addition.

1206 N. Cascade Avenue, c. 1895
(Courtesy Special Collections, Pikes Peak Library District.)

1230 N. Cascade Avenue

Architect E. C. G. Robinson designed this Colonial Revival style house in 1892 for mining broker William H. Tuttle. It features a hip roof with gabled dormers, wide boxed eaves, and a cornice with swag decoration. The full-width porch is supported by classical columns, and the front door has a leaded glass elliptical

1230 N. Cascade Avenue

fanlight and sidelights. The house once had a widow's walk on the roof and a balcony that extended the full width of the porch.

This c. 1899 photograph, taken during the annual flower carnival, shows 1230 N. Cascade Avenue in the background.
(Courtesy Denver Public Library, Western History Collection, H. S. Poley, Image P-2163.)

1308 N. Cascade Avenue

Wilfrid and Clarissa Hager built this brick Neoclassical style house in 1905. The Hagers were both from prominent Philadelphia banking families. They came to Colorado Springs seeking a cure for Wilfrid Hager's tuberculosis. The home was later owned by J. P. Shearer of the Perkins-Shearer Company. Designed

1308 N. Cascade Avenue

by architects Douglas & Hetherington, the house has a side gabled roof with wide eaves decorated with modillions. The façade is dominated by a full-height pedimented porch supported by massive classical columns.

The El Paso Canal

When Colorado Springs founder General William Jackson Palmer originally laid out the city, he realized that the downtown area's arid, parched, and treeless home lots would be difficult to sell. In order to attract new residents to the city, he wanted to beautify the streets with trees and vegetation. To accomplish this, water needed to be brought in for irrigation. In 1871, Palmer began construction on the El Paso Canal. It was an 11½-mile ditch that began at Fountain Creek in Old Colorado City and ended in Evergreen Cemetery. The canal began operation on November 28, 1872, and remained in use until 1956. Locals commonly referred to the canal as the "City Ditch."

This c. 1910 view of N. Cascade Avenue near Uintah Street shows the irrigation ditch in the lower right. Crossing the ditch required walking across narrow footbridges.
(Courtesy Colorado Historical Society, Image CHS.X5332.)

In the Old North End neighborhood, a series of lateral ditches carried water from the main canal at Columbia Street to the lots on Cascade, Nevada, Wahsatch, and Wood avenues. There is some evidence that there may have once been lateral ditches on Tejon and Weber streets as well. Remnants of the ditches can still be seen along portions of Cascade and Wood avenues. What appears to be a second sidewalk near the curb is actually a concrete slab covering the vacated irrigation ditches.

1332 N. Cascade Avenue

Designed by architect E. E. Neiman and built by contractor L. McKay, this Tudor style house was completed in 1930. W. E. McClung, president of the Newton Lumber Company in Colorado Springs, was the home's first owner. The house has a wood shingle roof, multiple front gables, stucco walls, and decorative half-

1332 N. Cascade Avenue

timbering. The oriel window in the primary gable and the elaborate brick chimneys are notable features of this house.

1424 N. Cascade Avenue

This charming Tudor style house was built in 1929 for Mrs. Rosie McColl, widow of Alex McColl. After her husband's death in 1914, she took over his business as a representative of the New York Life Insurance Company. She worked for the company for 36 years and won many of the firm's highest honors. Tudor

1424 N. Cascade Avenue

houses of a smaller size with whimsical features such as this one are often referred to as "Storybook Tudor" or "Fairy Tale" style. The wavy pattern seen in the roof shingles is intended to evoke the thatch roof houses of rural England. The patterned brickwork, bold half-timbering, and fanciful grapevine design on the vergeboards all contribute to the playful aesthetic.

1530 N. Cascade Avenue

Architect E. C. G. Robinson designed this grand Shingle style house in 1892. The home's first owner was John G. Shields, president and general manager of the Shields-Morley Grocery Company. He was also a director of First National Bank. The three-story house is cross-gabled, with a lower tower at the intersection

1530 N. Cascade Avenue

of the gables. Typical of the style, it has continuous wood shingle siding and overhanging gables with recessed windows. The estate's horse stable was converted to a residence in the 1950s and is now the house located at 11 W. Caramillo.

1530 N. Cascade Avenue, c. 1900
(Courtesy Special Collections, Tutt Library, Colorado College, Colorado Springs, Colorado.)

1600 N. Cascade Avenue

Arthur Sharp, former president of the Exchange National Bank, and his wife Louise built this striking house in 1913. In 1942, the home was purchased by the El Pomar Foundation, which then donated it to the American Red Cross. The building was used as the Red Cross chapter house until 2004. It has since been returned to

1600 N. Cascade Avenue

residential use. Designed by architect Nicholas Van den Arend, the house has a tile roof, brick walls, and a stone foundation. It exhibits Jacobean detailing with its Flemish style dormer, rounded arch arcade and stone trim. The porte-cochere on the north elevation is another interesting feature of this residence.

1700 N. Cascade Avenue

This elegant Tudor style house was built in 1930 as a summer residence for Oklahoma oil investor J. A. Chapman and his wife Leta. The two-story house has multiple front gables, a stone first story, and stucco with decorative half-timbering on the second story. It also features massive stone chimneys, gabled dormers, and leaded glass windows.

1700 N. Cascade Avenue

1730 N. Cascade Avenue

Designed by architect Thomas MacLaren and built by contractor R. E. Alderson, this Spanish Colonial Revival style house was competed in 1927. It was commissioned by E. C. Van Diest, a civil engineer who worked for General William Jackson Palmer in the construction of Glen Eyrie and Monument Valley Park. The

1730 N. Cascade Avenue

design features a tile roof, stucco walls, and casement windows. The façade is decorated with an arched stone door surround with a carved heraldic shield.

1818 N. Cascade Avenue

This Italian Renaissance Revival style house was built in 1915 for Jefferson Hayes Davis, grandson of Jefferson Davis, president of the Confederate States of America. Hayes-Davis was also vice president of the First National Bank. He and his wife Doree owned the residence until 1941. The hip roofed, two-story

1818 N. Cascade Avenue

house has a stucco-clad first story and wood shingle siding on the second story. The arched corbelled door hood is a unique feature of this notable house.

1908 N. Cascade Avenue

Architect F. E. Edbrook of Denver designed this impressive Shingle style house c. 1889. It was commissioned by millionaire Jerome B. Wheeler and built by contractor M. E. Mulloy. Mr. Wheeler was part owner of Macy's Department Store in New York City. He was also the developer of the Mollie Gibson

1908 N. Cascade Avenue

Mine and the Jerome Hotel and Opera House in Aspen, Colorado. The residence was later owned by C. C. Hemming, vice president of the El Paso National Bank. The design features a stone first story with wood shingle siding on the second and third stories. The steeply pitched front gable has a unique recessed

arch detail with an oriel window below. A low circular tower sits at the intersection of the gabled roof and a hip roof wing. The north elevation of the house has a gabled porte-cochere.

1908 N. Cascade Avenue, c. 1900
(Courtesy Special Collections, Pikes Peak Library District.)

1715 N. Cascade Avenue

1715 N. Cascade Avenue

This frame Queen Anne house was moved from its original location in the early 1900s. It was built c. 1896 for William J. Sawyer at the present site of the First Lutheran Church (1507 N. Cascade Avenue). While at its original location, it was also owned by Nelson B. Williams, owner of the Isabella Mining Company. William K. Jewett purchased the property at 1507 N. Cascade Avenue in 1900 and had the house moved to its current location. After the move, C. H. Curtis, president of the Curtis Coal Mining Company, and his wife Ethel occupied the house. It has an irregular roofline with gabled dormers, a prominent front-facing gable, and wood shingle siding. A large bow-front window on the second story sits above a full-width porch supported by turned columns.

1515 N. Cascade Avenue

1515 N. Cascade Avenue

Designed by architects Gove & Walsh, this Italian Renaissance Revival style house was built for William K. and Patty Jewett in 1902. Mr. Jewett was the vice president of Colorado Springs National Bank and was a mining investor. He is also known for purchasing the Colorado Springs Golf Club and donating it to the city. The course is now named after his wife Patty Jewett. In 1927, the home was sold to Ralph Giddings, owner of Giddings Department Store, formerly located on N. Tejon Street. The house is presently owned by the First Lutheran Church. It is constructed of gold colored brick with stone detailing and has a red tile hip roof with wide eaves. A prominent feature of the façade is the arcaded full-width porch. The north entrance is equally impressive with its round portico supported by classical columns.

1435 N. Cascade Avenue

This distinctive home was built c. 1902 by Henry LeB. Wills, president of the real estate firm Wills & Company, and his wife Caroline. It was later the long-time home of Russian immigrant Benjamin Lefkowsky, an artist and real estate developer. He was responsible for converting the Hagerman mansion at 610 N.

1435 N. Cascade Avenue

Cascade Avenue to apartments and built the Russ-Amer Arms Apartments (now Cascade Park Apartments) at 624 N. Cascade Avenue. He also developed the land to the west of these buildings as a residential area. The three-story wood frame house has an interesting mix of stylistic features, including a Craftsman style full-width front porch with oriental influences. The wide flared eaves

with exposed rafter tails are also typical Craftsman features. However, the home's large rectangular plan and prominent arched dormer are not commonly seen in the Craftsman style.

This c. 1905 photograph of 1435 N. Cascade Avenue shows that the three small windows in the arched dormer and the windows above the entry have since been replaced with larger windows. (Courtesy Special Collections, Pikes Peak Library District.)

2 E. Columbia Street

J. Arthur Connell, the first president of the Colorado Title & Trust Company, built this residence in 1900. It was designed by architects Douglas & Hetherington in the Elizabethan style. It has a side-gabled red tile roof with wide eaves and a stucco clad second story with decorative half-timbering. The first story is

2 E. Columbia Street

brick and features a square portico and a bay window on the façade. There is an enclosed porch on the west elevation.

2 E. Columbia Street, c. 1900. This view shows that the porch on the west elevation was once open, and the bay window on the façade was a later addition. (Courtesy Special Collections, Pikes Peak Library District.)

1325 N. Cascade Avenue

Architects Douglas & Hetherington designed this Shingle style house in 1902. Although the house has since been clad in stucco, it once had the continuous wood shingle siding that is typical of the style. It has a side-gambrel roof with a prominent gabled dormer on the façade. The full-width engaged

1325 N. Cascade Avenue

porch with stone piers is supported by a low stone wall that encloses the porch and wraps around to the south elevation where it connects to a stone portico. Windows are double-hung with a diamond pattern in the upper sash. The house was built for Edward W. Kent and his wife Annie. Mr. Kent was an employee at the Henry LeB. Wills & Co. real estate firm. The house was later owned for many years by W. F. Richards, treasurer of Assurance Savings & Loan Association and vice president of Colorado Springs National Bank.

This historic photograph of 1325 N. Cascade Avenue shows the original shingle siding and decorative half-timbering in the gabled dormer. (Courtesy Special Collections, Tutt Library, Colorado College, Colorado Springs, Colorado.)

1205 N. Cascade Avenue

This Colonial Revival house was built in 1894 by architect E. C. G. Robinson as his own residence. It was later purchased by Charles L. Tutt. Mr. Tutt was the owner of a real estate and insurance business but later went into a partnership with Spencer Penrose in a mining venture in Cripple Creek. Along with others, the two later

1205 N. Cascade Avenue

formed the Colorado-Philadelphia Reduction Company and the Utah Copper Company. The copper mine was the richest in the country and made Tutt a millionaire. Four generations of the Tutt family lived in the house until 1959, when it became the property of Colorado College. It is now named Tutt Alumni House and is used by the alumni for offices, meetings, and events. Architectural features include a hip roof with hip dormers and wide boxed eaves, stucco walls, and a full-width porch with a balcony above.

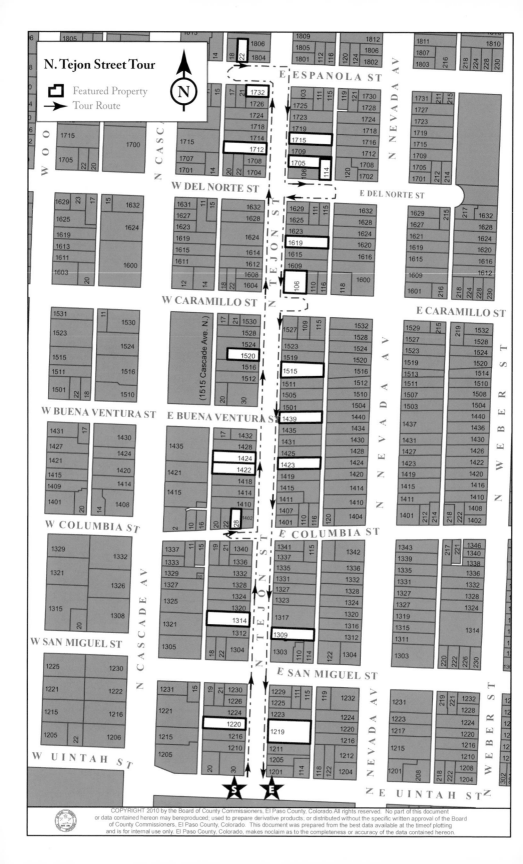

N. Tejon Street Tour

▢ Featured Property
→ Tour Route

N

Tour 4
N. Tejon Street

1300 block of N. Tejon Street, looking south, c. 1900
(Courtesy Special Collections, Pikes Peak Library District.)

Begin the tour at 1220 N. Tejon Street, just north of Uintah Street. The tour ends at 1219 N. Tejon Street. The distance of the tour is approximately 1.3 miles.

1220 N. Tejon Street

Built c. 1896, the first occupant of this Edwardian/Free Classic Queen Anne house was broker Fred J. Williams. It was later owned by dentist W. K. Sinton. The house has a side-gabled roof, wood shingle siding and a rounded wrap-around porch with classical columns. The second story of the façade has a cross-

1220 N. Tejon Street

gable with a small hip roof porch and an oriel window.

1314 N. Tejon Street

This two-story Craftsman style house was built in 1921 for Ira and Mary Conger. Mr. Conger owned an elevator business in Canada. The plan for this house was sold in a mail order house plan book titled *The Bungalow Book* by Henry L. Wilson. Building houses from this type of plan book was a common practice

1314 N. Tejon Street

in the early 1900s. In fact, the same plan was used to build the house located at 2026 N. Cascade Avenue. The two-story house has a side-gabled roof with wide eaves, exposed rafter tails, and a shed dormer. The façade has a gabled front porch with decorative half-timbering in the gable. It is supported by battered columns and stone piers.

28 E. Columbia Street

This Victorian Cottage was built in 1900 and features a cross-gabled roof, wood clapboard siding, and a full-width porch. The balcony above the porch is accessed by a projecting bay with French doors. The house was built for David Elliot, a state senator and managing editor of the *Colorado Springs Evening Telegraph* newspaper. ⚜

28 E. Columbia Street

1422 N. Tejon Street

Built c. 1901, this was the long-time home of Lulu and Roy A. Davis. He was a former city council member, Colorado speaker of the house, and state senator. He also owned the Davis Typewriter and Office Supply Company, formerly located on N. Tejon Street. The house has a hip roof with lower cross-gables. The

1422 N. Tejon Street

front-facing gable has a Palladian style window and fishscale shingles. A full-width porch with classical columns supports a large balcony above. A unique feature is the large oval shaped leaded glass window adjacent to the door.

1424 N. Tejon Street

Built c. 1890, this simple three-story Gable End Frame residence was the long-time home of Ira Harris, a district court judge and former mayor of Colorado Springs. The house is cross-gabled with wood shingle siding and a wrap-around porch with classical columns.

1424 N. Tejon Street

1520 N. Tejon Street

This Queen Anne style house was built c. 1892 and features a cross-gabled roof, wood shingle siding, and a full-width porch with a large corner turret. The first owner of the residence was John Campbell, who served as a city attorney, county attorney, state representative, state senator, and justice of the Colorado Supreme Court.

1520 N. Tejon Street

1712 N. Tejon Street

Built in 1902, this house was first occupied by Newman and Mary Crowley. Mr. Crowley was the owner of Star Laundry, formerly located downtown. From 1932 to 1950, it was the home of Jack Lawson, an editor at the *Colorado Springs Gazette* and a journalism instructor at Colorado College. The Hoyt family owned

1712 N. Tejon Street

the house from 1950 to 1963. Austin Hoyt served as district court judge in Colorado Springs and was later nominated by President John F. Kennedy as a judge of the U.S. tax court in Washington D.C. The Gable End Frame house has wood clapboard siding and a wrap-around porch. The façade features a Palladian window in the gable and an oriel window on the second story. The front door has an elliptical fanlight and sidelights. Several other windows in the home have leaded glass and beveled glass.

1732 N. Tejon Street

Attorney Rush L. Holland built this Colonial Revival style house in 1901. In 1921 he was appointed assistant attorney general of the United States. Features of the house include a flared hip roof with wide boxed eaves and wood clapboard siding. The façade has a full-width porch and balcony and an oriel window on the second story.

1732 N. Tejon Street

22 E. Espanola Street

Built c. 1900, this dwelling's earliest resident was George Bacon Price, a mechanical engineer. In 1911, Charles W. and Mary Howbert purchased the house. Mr. Howbert was part owner of the Robert E. Lee silver mine and manager of the Anchoria-Leland and Conundrum mines. He lived in

22 E. Espanola Street

the house until his death in 1950. The house has a steeply-pitched hip roof with boxed eaves. The large gable wall dormer on the façade has an arched window and fishscale shingles. Square columns and stone piers support a full-width front porch with a segmental arch over the entry.

The Old North End Neighborhood (ONEN) Plaque Program

While taking the walking tours of the Old North End, you may notice a number of houses with oval bronze plaques denoting the construction date. Many houses also have a second plaque with a brief history of the former occupants. These plaques are the result of the ONEN Plaque Program.

ONEN plaques at 2027 N. Tejon Street

Old North End resident Matt Railey initiated the program in 1986. After researching his own house at 2027 N. Tejon Street, he wrote a book entitled Sadie's House which chronicled his research experience and documented the fascinating history of his house. He proposed the idea of a plaque program to the North End Homeowners Association (now ONEN) and began teaching a house research class at Penrose Public Library. Once homeowners completed the research, they were eligible for the honorary bronze plaques. The program was later administered by ONEN's Historic Preservation Committee, chaired by Pat Doyle.

The plaque program has been very successful, both in encouraging homeowners to learn about the history of their houses and in contributing to the collective history of the Old North End neighborhood.

1715 N. Tejon Street

This charming Queen Anne house was built in 1901. An early resident was William S. Butler, an engineer at the Colorado Springs Light, Heat and Power Company. The house has a steeply pitched side-gabled roof with a gable wall dormer and an octagonal tower on the façade. The first story has wood clapboard siding, and the

1715 N. Tejon Street

second story has decorative fishscale shingles.

1705 N. Tejon Street

This c. 1874 Italianate style house was moved to this location from the site of the present Post Office at Nevada and Pikes Peak avenues. It functioned as a boarding house at its original location. After it was moved to this site, it was the long-time home of real estate broker William L. Gray and his wife Mary. Typical of the Italianate

1705 N. Tejon Street

style, it has a low pitch hip roof with a bracketed cornice. The segmental arched windows have surrounds with a fleur-de-lis detail. The iron fence enclosing the property was made at the Barnum Foundry of Detroit, Michigan.

114 E. Del Norte Street

Mrs. Roxie Brown, a widowed dressmaker, built this house in 1901. She was remarried in 1907 to Alexander Wiley, auditor of the Antlers Hotel. The couple occupied the house until 1914. In the 1930s it became the residence of Robert Wardwell and his wife Gladys, who lived in the house for over 50 years. Robert Wardwell

114 E. Del Norte Street

was the national advertising manager at the *Colorado Springs Gazette* and was later the postmaster of Colorado Springs. Gladys Wardwell was a prominent piano teacher. The house has a flared side-gabled roof with one large gable dormer and one small gable dormer on the façade. The full-width engaged porch has a closed rail and is supported by paired columns.

1619 N. Tejon Street

This Colonial Revival style house was built c. 1899 and was the home of the Wandell family for many years. H. V. Wandell was the president of the Wandell and Lowe Transfer and Storage Company. After his death in 1910, his wife Lillie and their children continued to live in the house for over 20 years. The

1619 N. Tejon Street

design features a hip roof and a large gable dormer with a small balconette on the façade. The porch is full-width with paired columns and a pediment above the entry. An elliptical fanlight and sidelights surround the front door.

106 E. Caramillo Street

This unique c. 1895 house has several features that are influenced by the Chateauesque style, which is a style loosely based on the 16th century chateaus of the French Loire Valley. The steeply-pitched hip roof and parapeted gable dormers of this house are typical of the style. However, formal Chateausque style buildings are

106 E. Caramillo Street

typically larger in scale and are of masonry construction. The home was once used as a boarding house and was later the long-time residence of Robert and Sarah Bensberg.

106 E. Caramillo Street, c. 1895
(Courtesy Special Collections, Pikes Peak Library District.)

1515 N. Tejon Street

Attorney Joseph W. Ady and his wife Louise built this c. 1900 Dutch Colonial Revival style house. Mr. Ady was formerly a politician in Kansas, serving in the Kansas House of Representatives and as the U.S. district attorney for that state. After his death in 1901, his wife Louise continued to live in the house until 1921.

1515 N. Tejon Street

The house has a complex roofline with both a front-facing gambrel and a front gable, each with decorative fishscale shingles. The classical partial-width front porch has a balustraded balcony above.

1439 N. Tejon Street

This 1900 cross-gabled Queen Anne was a rental property for many years. In the 1950s, it became the long-time home of Carlton Gamer, a composer and professor of music at Colorado College. The house features a square two-story corner tower with flared hip roof. The full-width porch has decorative spindlework and a small pediment over the entry.

1439 N. Tejon Street

1423 N. Tejon Street

Physician Gerald Webb was an early occupant of this c. 1896 Gable End Frame residence. Dr. Webb lived here from 1897 to 1901, and his medical office was also located in the house. He later became an acclaimed tuberculosis specialist. (See call-out, next page.) The house is cross-gabled with a tin roof, wood shingle siding, and a stone foundation. The overhanging front gable has a Palladian window, fishscale shingles, and a decorative swag detail. The first story has a gabled front porch and bay window with a similar swag detail.

1423 N. Tejon Street

Dr. Gerald Webb

Internationally renowned tuberculosis specialist and researcher Dr. Gerald Webb was a resident of the Old North End neighborhood for over 50 years. After living at 1423 N. Tejon Street from 1897 to 1901, he lived at 1222 N. Cascade Avenue until the late 1940s.

Born in Cheltenham, England, in 1871, he immigrated to Colorado in 1893 to attend

(Courtesy Special Collections, Tutt Library, Colorado College, Colorado Springs, Colorado.)

Denver University. He came to Colorado Springs in 1896, where he practiced medicine for 52 years, primarily in the field of tuberculosis treatment. In 1904, Dr. Webb was married to Varina Howell Davis Hayes. She was the granddaughter of Jefferson Davis, president of the Confederacy. The couple had four children.

Dr. Webb built an addition on his Cascade Avenue house to accommodate his own tuberculosis research laboratory. He quickly became one of the leaders in tuberculosis research in the United States and was delegated as a U.S. representative at several international tuberculosis conferences. He authored numerous books and pamphlets on tuberculosis and served as president of both the National Tuberculosis Association and the American Physicians Association. In 1924, Dr. Webb established the Colorado Foundation for Research in Tuberculosis at Colorado College.

Dr. Gerald Webb died at his Cascade Avenue home on January 27, 1948. After his death, his research institute was relocated from Colorado College to the Denver campus of the University of Colorado and is now known as the Webb-Waring Institute for Biomedical Research.

1309 N. Tejon Street

Optometrist George R. Bergen and his wife Nellie built this Craftsman style house in 1910. It was later the home of George M. LeCrone, president of the Democrat Publishing Company. The house has a hip roof with wide eaves and exposed rafter tails. The full-width porch is supported by battered columns

1309 N. Tejon Street

and extends across the driveway to form a porte-cochere. A flared gable with triangular brackets and decorative half-timbering is located above the porch entry. These same details are mirrored in each of the gable dormers.

1219 N. Tejon Street

This Gable End Frame house was built in 1887 for the Perkins family. W. Arthur Perkins was president of the Perkins-Shearer clothing store and lived in the house with his wife Emily for over 50 years. The home remained in the Perkins family for 83 years. The two-story house has a prominent front gable with a row

1219 N. Tejon Street

of three ribbon windows. The rounded wrap-around porch has a pediment over the entry and is supported by classical columns. The siding is wood clapboard with wood shingles in the gables. The original windows are double-hung and have multiple square panes in the upper sash.

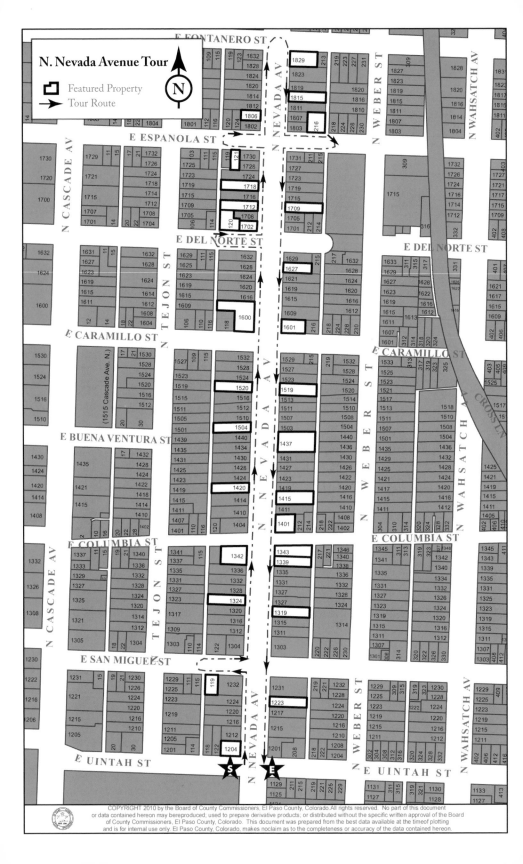

N. Nevada Avenue Tour

Featured Property
Tour Route

N

Tour 5
N. Nevada Avenue

1700 block of N. Nevada Avenue, looking south, 1927
(Photograph by Harry L. Standley, courtesy Special Collections, Pikes Peak Library
District. Image 102-10384.)

Begin the tour at the northwest corner of Nevada Avenue and Uintah Street. The tour ends at 1223 N. Nevada Avenue, just north of Uintah Street. The distance of the tour is approximately 1.5 miles.

1204 N. Nevada Avenue

Louisa M. Thrall, widow of Frank G. Thrall, built this brick Craftsman bungalow in 1922. It has a flared side-gabled tile roof with wide eaves and exposed rafter tails. The façade features a gable dormer and a full-width engaged porch with battered piers at each corner. This porch design allows for a single span without

1204 N. Nevada Avenue

intermediate supports, enabling an unrestricted view from the front windows.

119 E. San Miguel Street

This wood shingled Craftsman bungalow was constructed by builder A. D. W. Holman in 1920. He and his wife Julia owned the house until 1924. It was later the long-time home of Lester Howard, former principal of South Jr. High School, and his wife Glenn Howard, a voice teacher. The house is front-gabled

119 E. San Miguel Street

with large shed dormers and wide eaves supported by triangular brackets. The full-width engaged porch is partially enclosed with windows.

1324 N. Nevada Avenue

This three-story Shingle style house was built c. 1894. Typical of the style, it has continuous wood shingle siding and minimal decorative detail. The overhanging front gable and side cross gable both have fishscale shingles and eave returns. The engaged partial-width porch is supported by a square, shingled pier and has a

1324 N. Nevada Avenue

shingled closed rail. The house was built by Franklin E. Brooks, an attorney and a U. S. congressman from 1902 to 1907.

1342 N. Nevada Avenue

Alvaro Hemenway, a mining investor and grocery store owner, built this Edwardian/Free Classic Queen Anne c. 1896. The house was later owned by his son, O. E. Hemenway, who was vice president of Colorado Springs National Bank. His daughter, Addie, continued to live in the house until her death in 1968. The

1342 N. Nevada Avenue

design features a cross-gabled roof with multiple front gables and a prominent oriel window in the second story. Walls on the first story have wood shingle siding, and there are fishscale shingles on the second and third stories. The full-width porch with Craftsman style battered columns is not original to the house. The original porch, replaced in 1920, probably had classical features. ⚜

1420 N. Nevada Avenue

Photographer Charles Emery and his wife Bertha built this Queen Anne residence c. 1894. Emery's photographs included landscapes, buildings, and portraits of pioneer residents. Many of his photographs are now housed in various city archives. The hip roof house has small, hip dormers

1420 N. Nevada Avenue

and cross gables with fishscale shingles. The full-width porch originally wrapped around to the bay window on the south elevation but has since been modified.

This c. 1900 photograph of 1420 N. Nevada Avenue shows the original wrap-around porch.
(Courtesy Special Collections, Tutt Library, Colorado College, Colorado Springs, Colorado.)

1504 N. Nevada Avenue

Ira J. Morse, a wholesale produce dealer, and his wife Annie built this Queen Anne residence in 1901. The design features a cross-gabled roof with a flared front gable and a gable dormer. The house also exhibits some elements of the Shingle style, including the continuous wood shingle siding, the shingled brackets in the dormer, and the square shingled posts supporting the gabled portion of the wrap-around porch.

1504 N. Nevada Avenue

1520 N. Nevada Avenue

Built c. 1894, this half-timbered Queen Anne's earliest resident was G. B. Turnbull, former principal of Colorado Springs High School. It was later the home of William Strachan, a retired rancher, and his wife Jessie. The house has brick walls and decorative half-timbering and stucco in the front gables.

1520 N. Nevada Avenue

1600 N. Nevada Avenue

Designed in the Spanish Mission style, this 1924 house has the characteristic curvilinear parapet, red tile roof, and stucco walls. The arched entry porch and façade windows are also typical of the style. The house was built by Dr. W. A. Campbell, a physician and former chief of staff at Memorial Hospital.

1600 N. Nevada Avenue

120 E. Del Norte Street

The features of this unique house exhibit influences of both the Queen Anne and Colonial Revival styles. It was built in 1901 for Carlton and Anna Aylard, who were both school teachers. It was later the long-time home of the Strickler family. David P. Strickler was the attorney for the

120 E. Del Norte Street

W. S. Stratton estate and was president of the Board of Trustees of the Myron Stratton Home. The two-story hip roof residence has wood clapboard siding and an oriel window on the second story. A prominent feature of this house is the semi-circular portion of the porch on the east side of the façade, which is open on the first story and enclosed on the second story.

1702 N. Nevada Avenue

Dr. George Wilson and his wife Alice built this grand residence in 1905. Dr. Wilson was a dentist who practiced in Colorado Springs for 46 years. The three-story house has an interesting mix of stylistic features. Elements of the Tudor style can be seen in the steeply-pitched gable roof and the wrap-around porch with

1702 N. Nevada Avenue

Tudor arches. Other features, such as the wood clapboard wall cladding and the wood shingles in the gables, are not typical of the Tudor style. Classical detailing is exhibited in the windows and porch columns, and the Craftsman style is represented in the open eaves with exposed rafter tails.

1712 N. Nevada Avenue

This simple Gable End Frame residence was once the home of Artus and Anne Van Briggle, owners of the Van Briggle Pottery Company. Artus Van Briggle's funeral was held in the house when he died in 1904, as was Anne Van Briggle's wedding when she remarried in 1908. She and her new husband, mining

1712 N. Nevada Avenue

engineer Etienne A. Ritter, lived here until 1918. (See call-out, next page.) The house was built c. 1897 and has a cross-gabled roof and a hip roof wrap-around porch. The present siding material is not original.

Artus and Anne Van Briggle

World-renowned ceramic artist Artus Van Briggle is best known as the founder and former president of Van Briggle Pottery. However, he is also celebrated as an innovator in early 20th century American art pottery. He is credited with rediscovering the Chinese "dead glaze" technique, which had been lost to history since the Ming dynasty. The distinctive matte finish obtained with this method would later become the hallmark of Van Briggle Pottery designs.

Due to health problems associated with tuberculosis, Artus Van Briggle moved from Ohio to the drier climate of Colorado Springs in 1899. He opened Van Briggle Pottery in 1901 and married fellow artist Anne Gregory in 1902. The couple made their home at 1712 N. Nevada Avenue.

The Van Briggle Memorial Pottery, designed by architect Nicholas Van den Arend.
(Photograph by Knutson-Bowers Photography, courtesy Special Collections, Pikes Peak Library District. Image 001-9353.)

Anne Van Briggle collaborated with Artus in all aspects of the pottery business and was responsible for creating many of the company's designs. Their work quickly attained national and international acclaim and received numerous prestigious awards. However, as the pottery business thrived, Artus Van Briggle's health steadily deteriorated. He died in 1904 at the age of 35.

After his passing, Anne Van Briggle took over as president of the company. In 1908, the Van Briggle Memorial Pottery building was constructed at Uintah Street and Glen Avenue in Colorado Springs. Anne left the company in 1910 and later moved to Denver, where she died in 1929.

1718 N. Nevada Avenue

Assayer and chemist Edwin C. Woodward and his wife Annie built this Dutch Colonial Revival style residence in 1897 and owned it until 1928. The house has a cross-gambrel roof, wide cornices, and wood shingle siding. The façade features a classical wrap-around porch and a leaded glass entry door surround.

1718 N. Nevada Avenue

121 E. Espanola Street

This 1901 Classic Cottage features a flared hip roof and dormers, wood clapboard siding, and a full-width classical porch. The first residents of the house were Roger and Frances Scofield. Mr. Scofield was the superintendent of the Portland Mill, which processed gold ore from Cripple Creek.

121 E. Espanola Street

1806 N. Nevada Avenue

Built in 1901, this Shingle style house was the longtime residence of dressmaker Katherine Lucas. It has a gambrel roof with a large front cross-gable and a full-width porch. The continuous wood shingle siding, lack of decorative detail, and recessed windows in the gable are all typical features of the Shingle style.

1806 N. Nevada Avenue

1829 N. Nevada Avenue

Contractor Samuel Scholz built this Prairie style house in 1906 and lived in it until 1911. It then became the residence of Delina and Harry C. Chapman, president of the Giles Mercantile Company. Noted attorney Chester B. Horn and his wife Frances purchased the home in 1926 and owned it for many years. The hip roof, hip

1829 N. Nevada Avenue

dormers, and wide boxed eaves are typical features of the Prairie style. The full-width porch has been partially enclosed.

1815 N. Nevada Avenue

Contractor Samuel Scholz, who also built 1829 N. Nevada, built this Shingle style residence in 1902. He lived in the house until 1904, when it became the home of Fred and Mary Tucker, owners of the F. S. Tucker Furniture Company. The house has a gambrel roof with a large flared gable dormer with eave returns.

1815 N. Nevada Avenue

The full-width engaged porch is supported by massive stone columns and a stone closed rail.

216 E. Espanola Street

This Queen Anne residence was built in 1904. The design features a cross-gabled roof, an octagonal tower, and a pedimented front porch. The siding material is not original. In 1917, it became the long-time home of Charles C. Mierow and his wife Bernadine. Mr. Mierow was a professor at Colorado College and was president of the college from 1923 to 1934.

216 E. Espanola Street

1709 N. Nevada Avenue

Clement and Anna Barnes built this Craftsman bungalow in 1908. Mr. Barnes was president of the Barnes-Stephens Plumbing Company. The house was later the long-time residence of J. Harold and Edna Frantz. It is side-gabled with wide eaves and exposed rafter tails. There is a large gable dormer with decorative half-timbering on the façade. The full-width engaged porch has square columns and a closed rail.

1709 N. Nevada Avenue

1627 N. Nevada Avenue

This Colonial Revival style house was built in 1900. It has a symmetrical plan with a hip roof and hip dormers. The classically detailed full-width porch and balcony are prominent features of the façade. In 1901, Harry J. and Alice Newman purchased the house. Mr. Newman owned H. J. Newman & Company, a mining

1627 N. Nevada Avenue

investment firm. The Newman family lived in the home until 1956.

1601 N. Nevada Avenue

Built in 1898, this Edwardian/ Free Classic Queen Anne has a cross-gabled roof with multiple front gables. The walls are clad in wood clapboard, with fishscale shingles in the gables. It has a classical wrap-around porch with a pediment over the entry and a two-story bay window on the south elevation. The house

1601 N. Nevada Avenue

was built by John Henry Avery, who was secretary and treasurer of the Elkton Consolidated Mining and Milling Company.

1519 N. Nevada Avenue

Mining investor Henry H. Barbee built this c. 1897 Edwardian/Free Classic Queen Anne residence. By 1901, it was purchased by another mining investor, Charles W. Kurie, and his wife Mary. The façade features a two-story octagonal tower and a wrap-around porch that mimics the shape of the tower on the south

1519 N. Nevada Avenue

end. Other details include a gable dormer with a scroll detail, diamond pane windows, and a small oval window on the second story. Both the tower and a two-story bay window on the south elevation have a decorative swag detail.

1437 N. Nevada Avenue

This unique house was built in 1901 and has an interesting combination of architectural features. As seen in the photo below, the façade once had a full-width porch and balcony that have since been removed. The house has many elements of the Shingle style, including the irregular roofline, continuous

1437 N. Nevada Avenue

shingle siding, and an eyebrow dormer. The half-timbering in the octagonal tower, however, is not common in the Shingle style and was likely influenced by the contemporaneous Tudor style. In 1903, Edgar and Lulu Ullrich purchased

the house. Mr. Ullrich was the president of the El Paso Ice & Coal Co. and was later the general manager of the Utah Ice and Storage Company.

This c. 1901 photograph of 1437 N. Nevada Avenue shows the original porch and balcony.
(Courtesy Special Collections, Pikes Peak Library District.)

1415 N. Nevada Avenue

Architect T. D. Hetherington designed this Dutch Colonial Revival style residence c. 1888 for Colonel Edgar Ensign and his wife Lilla. Colonel Ensign was the former president of First National Bank, Assurance Savings & Loan, and Citizens State Bank. As the first state forest commissioner in Colorado, Ensign was appointed

1415 N. Nevada Avenue

by the U. S. government to lay out the majority of the United States forest reserves in the state. The house has a side gambrel roof with two prominent gambrel wall dormers on the façade. The first story is constructed of stone, and the second story has wood shingle siding. The façade also has a bay window and a small flat-roofed porch with paired square columns.

1401 N. Nevada Avenue

This charming Tudor bungalow was designed by architect Thomas MacLaren for financier Robert Rhea in 1924. Architectural features include a red tile roof, flared gables with decorative half-timbering, and stucco walls.

1401 N. Nevada Avenue

An early view of 1401 N. Nevada Avenue
(Courtesy Special Collections, Pikes Peak Library District. Image 044-9086.)

1343 N. Nevada Avenue

The former superintendent of Colorado Springs public schools, professor P. K. Pattison, built this Edwardian/Free Classic Queen Anne residence c. 1890. It was later the long-time home of high school teacher Willet R. Willis and his wife Annie. The house is cross-gabled and has wood shingle siding. Fishscale shingles

1343 N. Nevada Avenue

and vergeboards decorate the gables. The full-width porch has a round turret roof on the south end. The porch's battered columns are typically seen in the Craftsman or Prairie styles and are likely not original. ⚜

1339 N. Nevada Avenue

Built c. 1891, this Queen Anne style house was the longtime residence of John and Martha Lennox, who were both pioneer Colorado Springs residents. Although very similar in plan to the Free Classic Queen Anne next door, this house has spindlework ornamentation, which is more delicate and elaborate than the

1339 N. Nevada Avenue

detailing on Free Classic examples. This is especially evident in the intricate decoration in the two front gables and the narrow paired columns on the full-width porch.

1319 N. Nevada Avenue

Architects Pease and Barber designed this massive Dutch Colonial Revival style house for mining broker J. K. Miller in 1888. Beginning in 1913, the home was used as a Colorado College fraternity house for Alpha Tau Delta and later Phi Delta Theta. The building has since returned to private ownership and currently

1319 N. Nevada Avenue

contains multiple apartment units. The house has a cross-gambrel roof with wave pattern shingles in each gambrel. Small arched dormers located on the north and south elevations have a classical shell carving with decorative swags below. This

same detail is seen above the Palladian window in the front-facing gambrel. The façade has a wrap-around porch with a corner turret, paired ionic columns, and a pediment over the entrance.

1319 N. Nevada Avenue, c. 1900
(Courtesy Special Collections, Pikes Peak Library District.)

1223 N. Nevada Avenue

This Edwardian/Free Classic Queen Anne is hip-roofed with lower cross gables and a round two-story corner tower. The walls are sided with wood shingles and have decorative fishscale shingles in the gables. The façade has a wrap-around porch with a small pediment over the entry. The house was built c. 1898 for

1223 N. Nevada Avenue

Edward F. and Henrietta Woestman, owners of the Cascade Ice Company.

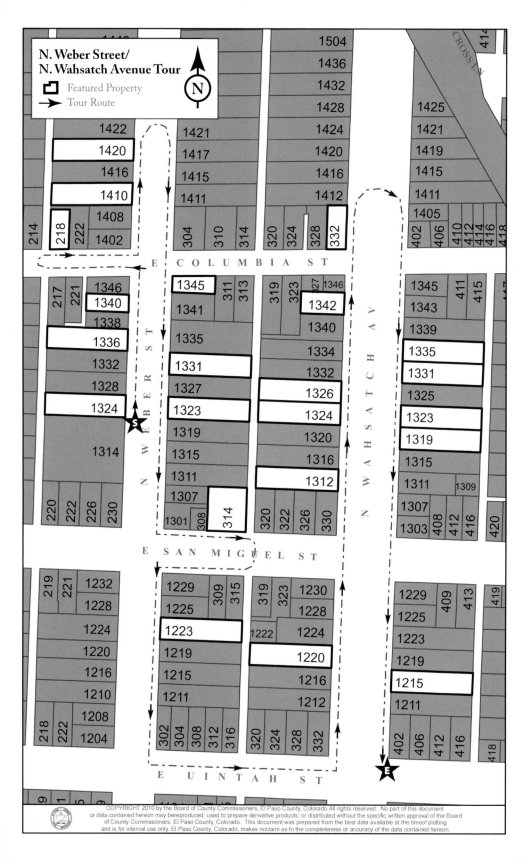

N. Weber Street/
N. Wahsatch Avenue Tour

☐ Featured Property
→ Tour Route

N

Tour 6

N. Weber Street/
N. Wahsatch Avenue

1300 block of N. Wahsatch Avenue, looking south, c. 1920
(Photograph by Harry L. Standley, courtesy Special Collections, Pikes Peak Library
District. Image 102-10388.)

Begin the tour at 1324 N. Weber Street, just north of E. San Miguel Street. The tour ends at 1215 N. Wahsatch Avenue, just north of Uintah Street. The distance of the tour is approximately 1 mile.

1324 N. Weber Street

Contractor Isaac Marker and his wife Lulu built this cross-gabled bungalow in 1910 and lived in the house for two years. It was later the home of Augustus and Zella Moseley. The cross-gabled house has wood shingle siding, wide eaves, and exposed rafter tails. The full-width porch has square columns and a closed shingled rail.

1324 N. Weber Street

1336 N. Weber Street

This brick apartment building has a flat roof and a projecting full-width two-story porch with square brick columns and a closed brick rail. It was built in 1913 by contractor R. F. Schmitt, who also owned the building. The cost of construction was just $8,000.

1336 N. Weber Street

1340 N. Weber Street

Frank C. Jordan, a teacher at Colorado Springs High School (now Palmer High School), built this Edwardian/Free Classic Queen Anne in 1903. It was later the residence of Samuel and Mabel Kinsley. Mr. Kinsley was a former Colorado Springs city attorney and an El Paso County judge. The cross-gabled house has

1340 N. Weber Street

wood clapboard siding with fishscale shingles in the gables. The porch is full-width and has classical columns and a pediment over the entry.

218 E. Columbia Street

Architect T. D. Hetherington of the firm Douglas & Hetherington designed this charming bungalow as his own residence in 1900. (See call-out, next page.) It was later the long-time home of T. D. Hetherington's daughter, Mrs. W. J. Honeyman. The house has a cross-gabled roof, wood shingle siding, and decorative

218 E. Columbia Street

half-timbering in the gable. The stone full-width porch has a stone archway at the entrance and is supported with both square columns and stone piers.

218 E. Columbia Street, c. 1900. Note that the higher gable on the east elevation is a later addition. (Courtesy Special Collections, Pikes Peak Library District.)

1410 N. Weber Street

This unique Shingle style house was built c. 1900 for widow Hattie H. Wheeler. In 1904, it was purchased by long-time owner James J. Eubank, manager of the Russell Gates Mercantile Company. The design features a side-gabled roof, stone walls on the first story, and wood shingle siding on the second story. The

1410 N. Weber Street

most prominent feature of the house is the two-story stone tower located at the southeast corner. The partial-width engaged porch is supported by both classical columns and a square stone pier.

Architects Douglas & Hetherington

The highly regarded architectural firm of Douglas & Hetherington (1896-1914) was well known for the many prominent buildings that the company designed in Colorado Springs. These included several downtown commercial blocks, Ticknor and McGregor Halls at Colorado College, and the now demolished Burns Building and Theater. They also designed numerous stately residences, many of which are located in the Old North End neighborhood.

2 E. Columbia Street, designed by architects Douglas & Hetherington
(Courtesy Special Collections, Pikes Peak Library District.)

The firm was comprised of Walter F. Douglas and T. Duncan Hetherington. Mr. Douglas was a University of Edinburgh graduate who came to Colorado Springs in 1888 and began working as an independent architect. In 1896, Mr. Hetherington relocated to Colorado Springs from Denver, where he had been working in the office of architect Robert S. Roeschlaub. Douglas and Hetherington opened their firm that same year. Their successful partnership lasted for 18 years. When Mr. Douglas left Colorado Springs in 1914, Mr. Hetherington went into partnership with well-known architect Thomas MacLaren.

Residences designed by Douglas & Hetherington are noted in walking tours 2, 3, 5 and 6.

1420 N. Weber Street

Built c. 1896, this home's first resident was bookkeeper W. H. R. Stote and his wife Florence. By 1898, Henry H. and Lizzie Cooper occupied the residence. Mr. Cooper was involved in mining and also owned a grocery store. The couple later lived at 1220 N. Wahsatch Avenue for many years. The house

1420 N. Weber Street

is a cross-gabled cottage with some Queen Anne features, including the turned porch columns and the fishscale shingles in the gables.

1420 N. Weber Street, c. 1896
(Photograph by Charles E. Emery, courtesy Special Collections, Pikes Peak Library District. Image 001-6112.)

1345 N. Weber Street

This bungalow was built in 1902 and was for many years the home of Amanda and Emma Simkins. Amanda was the widow of William Simkins and Emma was a teacher at Lowell School. The cross-gabled roof has wide eaves and exposed rafter tails. The double-hung windows have 4-over-1 sash, and the full-width

1345 N. Weber Street

porch has paired square columns. A lunette window decorates the gable over the porch entrance. Interestingly, the house located at 1705 N. Nevada Avenue is nearly identical to this house in plan.

1331 N. Weber Street

Lewis B. and Olive Skinner built this Colonial Revival style house in 1902. In 1904, it became the long-time residence of Harold C. and Mary B. Harmon. Mr. Harmon was the president of the Colorado Springs Fuel Company. The house is hip-roofed with gable dormers. The full-width porch is partially enclosed and has classical columns. Other Colonial Revival features include the dentil molding at the cornice, the corner pilasters, and windows with diamond paned upper sash.

1331 N. Weber Street

1323 N. Weber Street

Insurance salesman William Jonson built this two-story Craftsman house in 1912 at a cost of $3,500. It is side-gabled with wide eaves and exposed rafter tails. Triangular brackets and fishscale shingles decorate the gables. The full-width shed roof porch has brick piers with square columns.

1323 N. Weber Street

314 E. San Miguel Street

Fire Station No. 2 was built in 1939 to replace the original station No. 2, which was built on this site in 1896. Architect Earle Deits designed this building to be compatible with the bungalows and smaller houses on the street. The one-story Spanish Colonial style building has a Spanish tile cross-gabled roof and brick walls.

314 E. San Miguel Street

The façade features an octagonal tower with a wide band of decorative tile work at the cornice. The two garage doors are segmentally arched with stone surrounds, and the gables have quatrefoil windows with decorative iron grills.

1223 N. Weber Street

This Craftsman bungalow was built in 1905 and features a front gable with half-timbering and a full-width porch with a stone closed rail. The house was built for H. V. Holman, secretary and treasurer of Gem Toilet & Laundry. It was later the residence of H. J. Nathan and his wife Minnie. Mr. Nathan was

1223 N. Weber Street

the owner of Nathan's clothing store, formerly located downtown on Huerfano Street (now Colorado Avenue).

1220 N. Wahsatch Avenue

F. E. Stratton, owner of Colorado Springs Cycle Company, built this shingled bungalow in 1902. In 1906, it became the home of Henry and Lizzie Cooper. Mr. Cooper was a former grocery store owner and a mining investor. Lizzie Cooper died in 1916, and Henry Cooper continued to live

1220 N. Wahsatch Avenue

in the house until his death in 1924. The bungalow is cross-gabled with eave returns and gable dormers. The full-width hip roof porch has square shingled columns and a closed shingled rail.

1312 N. Wahsatch Avenue

This stucco Craftsman bungalow has a cross-gabled roof with clipped gables and wide eaves. A single battered pier supports the partial-width flat roofed porch. The house was built in 1923, and Roy and Katherine Harden were its first residents. Mr. Harden was the manager of the Home

1312 N. Wahsatch

Market Company. It was later the home of police officer Robert Wraith and his wife Lillian.

1324 N. Wahsatch Avenue

Service station owner William Beard and his wife Carrie built this Craftsman bungalow in 1921. Carrie Beard wrote and published a book in 1964 titled *Colorado Gold Rush Days*. The house is front-gabled and has wood shingle siding. The dramatic full-width porch features a single open span supported by battered piers at each corner.

1324 N. Wahsatch Avenue

1326 N. Wahsatch Avenue

Contractor T. J. Wright built this Craftsman bungalow in 1922 and lived in it for two years. It was later the long-time home of Arthur B. and Jean Chambers. Mr. Chambers was president of the Acme Ticket Company, and his wife Jean was secretary-treasurer of the business. The house is cross-gabled with bracketed eaves and exposed rafter tails. The porch roof extends across the driveway to form a charming porte-cochere with square brick supports.

1326 N. Wahsatch Avenue

1342 N. Wahsatch Avenue

Architect Thomas MacLaren designed this hip roof bungalow in 1902. The house has wide boxed eaves and wood shingle siding. The engaged porch has classical columns and a closed shingled rail. There is a second enclosed porch on the south elevation. The house was built for

1342 N. Wahsatch Avenue

James Strachan and his wife Florence. Mr. Strachan was a bookkeeper at First National Bank.

332 E. Columbia Street

This stucco Craftsman bungalow features a front-gabled roof with exposed rafter tails. The gables are decorated with triangular eave brackets, and the porch gable has decorative half-timbering. Battered columns support the closed rail porch. The house was built in 1924 for jeweler F. E. Funk and his wife Grace. Mr.

332 E. Columbia Street

Funk was a partner in the Mahan Jewelry Company, formerly located on E. Pikes Peak Avenue.

1335 N. Wahsatch Avenue

Carpenter William Risher built this one-story Craftsman bungalow in 1921 and lived in it with his wife Etta until 1923. It then became the home of E. V. Elliot and his wife Estella. Mr. Elliot was the proprietor of the Canteen Cigar Store. The house has a low-pitched front-gabled

1335 N. Wahsatch Avenue

roof and wood shingle siding. The partial-width gabled porch is supported by squat, square, tapered columns, often referred to as elephantine columns.

1331 N. Wahsatch Avenue

Built by tailor George Gatterer and his wife Nora in 1911, this front-gabled Craftsman bungalow has wide eaves with triangular brackets. The full-width engaged porch is supported by square grouped columns and brick piers. A unique feature of this house is the bracketed

1331 N. Wahsatch Avenue

decorative framing around the gable window.

1323 N. Wahsatch Avenue

William and Mary Macy, owners of Macy's Pharmacy, built this striking Craftsman bungalow in 1910. The cost of construction was just $3,000. The steeply-pitched cross-gabled roof has wide eaves and triangular eave brackets, and the front gable features a unique arched porch with a bowed closed

1323 N. Wahsatch Avenue

rail. The south elevation has a brick chimney with decorative clinker bricks and a shed roof bay window.

1319 N. Wahsatch Avenue

This c. 1911 Craftsman bungalow was the long-time home of Colorado Springs High School teacher Marjorie W. Dearing. The house has a front-gabled roof with triangular eave brackets and wood shingle siding. The partial-width gabled porch is supported by square columns and a stone

1319 N. Wahsatch Avenue

closed rail. The double hung windows have multiple lights in the upper sash.

1215 N. Wahsatch Avenue

Another fine example of the Craftsman style, this bungalow was built in 1922 for James and Margaret Desmond. Mr. Desmond was a baker at the Sanitary Baking Company. The house has stucco walls and a front-gabled roof. The gabled porch has brick piers and a brick closed rail.

1215 N. Wahsatch Avenue

The grouping of five ribbon windows in the porch area is an interesting feature of the façade.

Steele School

Steele School, located at 1720 N. Weber Street, has been an Old North End neighborhood fixture for over 100 years. The school was named for Benjamin W. Steele, an early editor of the *Colorado Springs Gazette*. The original two-story brick school building was designed by prominent architect Thomas MacLaren and was completed in 1901. The design was award winning, and a model of the school was placed in the Smithsonian Institution.

The original Steele School building in 1915 (Photograph by Harry L. Standley, courtesy Special Collections, Pikes Peak Library District. Image 001-451.)

By the early 1970s, the District 11 Board of Education determined that the building was no longer sufficient for their needs. The historic school was demolished in 1972, and construction began on a new, modern building. In stark contrast to the original building, the new school was designed with virtually no windows or skylights. Strong protests from Old North End residents convinced the board to add a number of windows.

Because Steele School had the second smallest playground in District 11, the Old North End Neighborhood (ONEN) initiated a campaign to create a park on the south side of the school property in the mid-1990s. Following the approval of Colorado Springs City Council, Del Norte Street was blocked off between Weber Street and the alley between Weber Street and Nevada Avenue. Steele School parents, students, and Old North End residents raised the $83,000 needed for construction, and a new park and gazebo were built on the site in 1997.

Glossary Of Terms

ADDITION- New construction added to an existing building or structure.

ARCADED WING WALL- A wall projecting from the main building that contains an arched opening.

ARCADED ENTRY PORCH- A porch comprised of a series of arches supported by columns, pillars, or piers.

ARCHED- A curved structural member used to span an opening.

BALCONETTE- An ornamental railing around the lower portion of a window that projects slightly to form a false balcony.

BALCONY- A platform that projects from a wall above ground level that is cantilevered or supported by columns or brackets. It is normally constructed in front of windows or doors and has a railing or balustrade.

BALUSTRADE- A series of balusters connected by a handrail, used on staircases, balconies, porches, etc.

BATTERED COLUMN/PIER- A column or pier that is thicker at the bottom than at the top.

BAUHAUS- A German school of design that became the birthplace of the modernist movement.

BAY WINDOW- A projecting window with an angular plan.

BELTCOURSE- A raised horizontal band of brick, stone, or wood used on the exterior of a building to delineate floor levels or to break up large expanses of wall surface. It is also referred to as a stringcourse.

BEVELED GLASS- A pane of glass with a decorative edge that is polished at an angle.

BLIND ARCH- A decorative arch with no opening that is engaged or attached to a wall.

BOWED WINDOW- A projecting window with a semicircular plan.

BOXED EAVES- That part of a roof that projects beyond the exterior wall and is enclosed by boards and/or moldings so that the rafters are not visible.

BRACKET- Support members found under eaves or other overhangs, which may be plain or decorated.

CANTILEVER- A horizontal member projecting from a wall without any supports along its projection.

CAPITAL- The top portion of a column or pillar.

CASEMENT WINDOW- A window sash that opens on hinges attached to its vertical edge.

CAST IRON- Iron that has been shaped by being melted and cast in a mold.

CHARACTER- The distinctive qualities and attributes of any element, structure, site, street, or district.

CLAPBOARD- Horizontal wooden boards used as a siding material that are tapered at the top and laid so that the thin edge is overlapped by the thick edge of the board above.

CLINKER BRICK- An overbaked brick that is misshapen or discolored, often used for creating visual interest in chimneys, porch supports, and walls.

CLIPPED GABLE- A gabled roof that is truncated near the peak to form a small hip. Also known as a jerkinhead roof.

CLOSED RAIL- A railing that is solid in appearance, without a balustrade. It is often constructed of the same material as the exterior walls or foundation, or clad in the same siding material.

COLUMN- A pillar, usually circular in plan.

CORBEL- A projecting architectural element, often carved or molded, which acts as a means of support for a roof beam.

CORINTHIAN- A classical order characterized by fluted columns with ornate capitals decorated with acanthus leaves.

CORNERBOARDS- Narrow vertical boards at the corner of exterior walls that protect the ends of clapboards.

CORNICE- Any projecting molding along the top of a wall or building.

CROSS GABLE/GAMBREL- A roofline in which two gable or gambrel roof forms intersect at a right angle.

DENTIL- A series of small square decorative blocks found on cornices.

DORMER WINDOW- A window that projects from a roof.

DOUBLE-HUNG WINDOW- A window with two moveable sashes.

EAVE- The edge of a roof that projects over an exterior wall.

EAVE BRACKET- A projecting support member found under eaves.

EAVE RETURN- An eave that is carried a short distance onto the gable end of a building. Also called a cornice return.

ELEVATION- Any one of the external faces of a building.

ELLIPTICAL- Having the shape of a geometric ellipse.

ENGAGED PORCH- A porch in which the roof is a continuation of the main roof of the building.

ENTABLATURE- In classical architecture, the horizontal section carried on columns or pilasters and comprised of a cornice, frieze, and architrave.

EYEBROW DORMER- A curved low dormer with no sides.

FAÇADE- The front or main elevation of a building.

FANLIGHT- A semicircular or fan shaped window usually found over entrance doors.

FINIAL- An ornament that caps a hip, gable, or pinnacle.

FISHSCALE SHINGLES- Small wood shingles with straight sides and rounded bottoms.

FLARED ROOF- A roof that curves upwards at the eaves.

FLEUR-DE-LIS- A decorative design element that resembles three leaves bound together by a band.

FLUTE- Vertical concave channels in column shafts, pilasters, or other surfaces.

FOUNDATION- The part of a structure that is in direct contact with the ground and serves to transmit the load of the structure to the earth.

FRIEZE- Any plain or decorative band or board on the top of a wall immediately below the cornice.

FULL-HEIGHT PORCH- A porch rising the full height of a building.

FULL-WIDTH PORCH- A porch spanning the entire width of a building.

GABLE- The triangular end of an exterior wall in a building with a ridged roof.

GABLE END /GABLE FRONT- A house type in which the gable is facing the street.

GABLE ROOF- A sloping roof that terminates in a gable. Also called a pitched roof.

GLAZING- Fitted glass in windows and doors.

HALF-TIMBERING- A method of construction in which the spaces between structural timbers are filled with brickwork or plaster. The same decorative effect is often achieved by applying wood timbers superficially to a wall surface.

HERALDIC SHIELD- A shield containing a coat of arms.

HIP ROOF- A roof formed by four pitched roof surfaces.

HOOD- A decorative and/or protective cover found over doors and windows.

IONIC COLUMN- A classical order characterized by column capitals with opposing spiral designs (volutes).

KEYSTONE- A wedge shaped stone located at the center of an arch.

LEADED GLASS- Small panes of clear or colored glass that are joined together using lead strips.

LIGHT- A pane of glass in a window or a glazed component of a window.

LOGGIA- A covered gallery or corridor that is open on at least one side and supported by columns or pierced openings in a wall.

LUNETTE WINDOW- A semicircular window.

MAINTAIN- To keep in an existing state of preservation and repair.

MASONRY- Constructed of stone, brick, concrete block, or tile.

MEDALLION- A circular ornament.

MODILLION- Ornamental blocks used to support a cornice.

MOLDING- A decorative band used for ornamentation and finishing, generally used in cornices or as trim around openings.

MULLIONS- A large vertical member separating two window casements or multiple windows.

MULTI-LIGHT WINDOW- A window sash with more than one pane of glass.

OCULUS WINDOW- A circular window.

ORIEL WINDOW- A bay window located above the first story.

PANE- A single piece of window glass, also known as a light.

PALLADIAN WINDOW- A three-part window consisting of a central arched sash flanked by narrower square or rectangular sash on either side. Also called a serliana.

PARAPET- A low wall or protective railing often used around a balcony or along the edge of a roof.

PARTIAL WIDTH PORCH- A porch spanning only a portion of a building.

PATERA- A small round oval disk or medallion that may be simple or elaborately decorated.

PATTERNED BRICKWORK- Brickwork formed into a pattern through the use of bricks of two or more colors or textures.

PEDIMENT- A triangular section used as a crowning element over structures, doors and windows.

PICKET- A pointed stake arranged vertically to create a fence.

PIER- Vertical supporting members that frame an opening such as a window or door.

PILASTER- A flat or half round decorative element that is applied to a wall suggesting a column.

PILLAR- Upright members used for supporting superstructures.

PITCH- The degree of the slope of a roof.

PLANK SHUTTERS- Shutters constructed of heavy, wide pieces of timber.

PLANK SIDING- A type of wood siding that consists of long, heavy pieces of timber that are typically wider and thicker than clapboard.

PORTE COCHERE- A covered entrance that projects across a driveway and is wide enough for wheeled vehicles to pass through.

PORTICO- A covered walkway or porch supported by columns or pillars.

POST- A vertical isolated upright used to support a superstructure.

PRESERVATION- Saving from destruction or deterioration.

QUATREFOIL WINDOW- A window with four lobes (foils).

QUOINS- Large rectangular stones, bricks or blocks that are laid vertically and used to decorate and/or reinforce the corners of a building.

RAFTER TAILS- The portion of a sloping roof member that projects beyond the wall.

REHABILITATION- Returning a structure to a viable use while preserving its distinctive architectural and historic character.

REMODELING- Altering a building without regard to its historic character and/or defining features.

RIBBON WINDOWS- A row of windows in a continuous horizontal band, separated only by mullions.

SASH- The framework of a window in which the panes of glass are set.

SCALE- The size and mass of a building's form in relation to nearby buildings.

SHED ROOF- A roof with one inclined plane. Also called a pent roof.

SEGMENTAL ARCH- An arch formed by the segment of a circle, or an arc.

SIDE-GABLED- A house type in which the gable is facing a side elevation.

SIDELIGHT- A narrow window beside an exterior door.

SIDING- The exterior wall covering or sheathing of a structure.

SIGNIFICANT- Having particularly important associations within the contexts of architecture, history and/or culture.

SPINDLEWORK- Decorative wood ornaments often used in gable trim, porches and staircases.

STAINED GLASS WINDOW- A window composed of pieces of colored glass that are typically attached with lead strips or solder.

STUCCO- A durable finish for exterior walls, usually composed of cement, sand, and lime.

SURROUND- The molded trim around a door or window opening.

SWAG- A decoration resembling a piece of draped cloth.

TOWER- A structure of greater height than width. May be free-standing or part of another building.

TRANSOM- A small window or series of panes above a door.

TUDOR ARCH- A low, wide arch with a flattened point.

TURNED COLUMN- A column that is shaped with a lathe.

TURRET- A small tower, often located at the corner of a building.

VERGEBOARD- A decorative board suspended from the incline of a gable roof. Also called a bargeboard.

WALL DORMER- A dormer whose face is on the same plane as the wall below and breaks the line at the cornice of a building.

WIDOW'S WALK- A railed rooftop platform.

WOOD SHINGLE SIDING- A siding material, typically manufactured from cedar, which may be laid in a regular or irregular pattern.

WRAP-AROUND PORCH- A porch that is attached to two or more sides of a building.

WROUGHT IRON- Iron that is rolled or hammered into shape.

Index

Acme Ticket Company, 133

Ady, Joseph W., 104

Ady, Louise, 104

Alamo Avenue, 18, 37, 47, 53-57

Alderson, R. E., 87

Aldrich, Sherwood, 60

Aldridge Mercantile Company, 50

Aldridge, Robin P., 50

Alexander Aircraft, 70

Alexander Film Company, 70

Alexander, J. Don, 70

Aley Drug Company, 55

Aley, Daisy, 55

Aley, Hamilton, 55

All Souls Unitarian Church, 73

Alpha Tau Delta, 123

American Physicians Association, 106

American Red Cross, 53, 86

Anchoria-Leland Mine, 100

Arkansas-Vancouver Timber and Lumber Company, 69

Arnold, Irene, 55

Arnold, Joseph, 55

Arts and Crafts movement, 43

Assurance Savings & Loan Association, 92, 121

Automobiles, 19

Avery, John Henry, 119

Aylard, Anna, 113

Aylard, Carlton, 113

Bancroft, George, 49

Barbee, Henry H., 120

Barber & Hastings, 25, 82

Barnes, Anna, 118

Barnes, Clement, 118

Barnes-Stephens Plumbing Company, 118

Barnum Foundry, 102

Battle Mountain, 78

Bauhaus movement, 52, 141

Beadles, Mildred, 57

Beadles, Robert, 57

Beard, Carrie, 133

Beard, William, 133

Bemis, Judson, 62, 63

Bennett, Charles P., 67

Bennett, Jane Quackenbush, 48

Bennett-Schellenberger Realty, 67

Bensberg, Robert, 104

Bensberg, Sarah, 104

Bergen, George R., 107

Bergen, Nellie, 107

Beth-El Hospital, 70

Betty, A. J., 49

Blackman, Alfred A., 70

Boston Department Store, 56, 57

Broadmoor Art Academy, 74

Broadmoor Polo Association, 52

Brooks, Franklin E., 111

Brown, Roxie, 103

Buena Ventura Street, 34, 74

Bungalow, 24, 43, 44, 71, 74, 96, 110, 118, 121, 126, 127, 129, 131-137

Bunts, Edward, 54

Burns Theater, 78, 128

Burns, Gladys Helen, 78

Burns, James F., 77, 78

Burns, James F., Jr., 78

Buses, 15

Butler, William S., 102

Cable, R. R., 67

Cache La Poudre Street, 10, 14

Campbell, John, 98

Campbell, W.A., 113

Canteen Cigar Store, 135

Cape Cod style, 48, 54

Caramillo Street, 55, 72, 86, 104

Carlson, C. A., 48, 55, 56

Cascade Avenue, 10-12, 15-19, 23-26, 33, 35, 36, 38, 63, 78, 80-90, 92, 93, 96, 106

Cascade Ice Company, 123

Cascade Park Apartments, 90

Chambers, Arthur B., 133

Chambers, Jean, 133

Chapman, Delina, 117

Chapman, Harry C., 117

Chapman, J. A., 87

Chapman, Leta, 87

Chateauesque, 104

Chief Theater, 78

Citizens State Bank, 121

City Auditorium, 51

City Beautiful movement, 16

Claremont, 51

Colonial Revival style, 31, 34-36, 39, 48, 53, 60, 70, 72, 74, 76, 83, 93, 99, 103, 113, 119, 130

Colorado College, 10, 11, 13-15, 60, 61, 63, 68, 70, 75, 93, 99, 105, 106, 118, 123, 128

Colorado College Museum, 72

Colorado Historical Society, 7, 20

Colorado Midland Railway Company (see also Midland Railroad), 64

Colorado Savings Bank of Colorado Springs, 57

Colorado Springs City Council, 14, 19, 21, 53, 97, 75, 138

Colorado Springs City Hall, 51

Colorado Springs Cycle Company, 132

Colorado Springs Day Nursery, 63, 72

Colorado Springs Evening Telegraph, 97

Colorado Springs Fine Arts Center, 63

Colorado Springs Fuel Company, 130

Colorado Springs Gas & Electric Company, 76

Colorado Springs Gazette, 63, 71, 82, 99, 103, 138

Colorado Springs Golf Club, 89

Colorado Springs High School, 15, 126, 136

Colorado Springs Light, Heat, and Power Company, 102

Colorado Springs National Bank, 66, 89, 92, 111, 113

Colorado Title & Trust Company, 91

Colorado Title and Abstract Company, 53

Colorado-Philadelphia Reduction Company, 93

Columbia Street, 17, 20, 47, 57, 84, 91, 97, 127, 128, 134

Columbian Exposition, 38, 40

Conger, Ira, 96

Conger, Mary, 96

Connell, J. Arthur, 91

Consumption, 12

Conundrum Mine, 100

Cooper, Albert, 49

Cooper, Fern, 49

Cooper, Henry H., 129, 132

Cooper, Lizzie, 129, 132

Corley Mountain Highway, 68

Corley, W. D., 68

Cottage, 24, 44, 97, 116, 129

Craftsman style, 39, 43, 69, 79, 90, 96, 107, 110, 111, 114, 118, 122, 130-137

Cripple Creek, 10-12, 17, 66, 77, 78, 93, 116

Crowley, Mary, 99

Crowley, Newman, 99

Culebra Avenue, 18, 47, 48, 50

Culebra Place, 41, 48, 49, 50

Cummings, Charley K., 62

Curtin, Thomas, 70

Curtis, C. H., 89

Curtis, Ethel, 89

Cutis Coal Mining Company, 89

Davie, Robert P., 69

Davie, Martha, 69

Davie Realty Company, 69

Davie Building & Investment Company, 69

Davis Typewriter and Office Supply Company, 97

Davis, Doree, 88

Davis, Jefferson, 88, 106

Davis, Jefferson Hayes, 88

Davis, Lulu, 97

Davis, Roy A., 97

Dearing, Marjorie W., 136

Deits, Earle, 131

Del Norte Street, 20, 32, 40, 49, 54, 68, 103, 113, 138

Democrat Publishing Company, 107

Denver, 9, 10, 20, 61, 71, 88, 115, 128

Denver University, 106

Dern Company, 48

Dern, Joseph J., 48

Desmond, James, 137

Desmond, Margaret, 137

Dickey, C. C., 82

District 11 Board of Education, 138

Dodge, Norma W., 53, 71

Dodge, Stuart P., 53, 71

Donaldson, Anne, 74

Donaldson, David V., 74

Douglas & Hetherington (see also Hetherington, T. D.), 25, 60, 69, 72, 75, 77, 79, 83, 91, 92, 127, 128

Doyle, James, 78

Doyle, Pat, 21, 101

Dunwoody, E. E., 73

Durkee, Charles E., 69

Durkee, Rose M., 68, 69

Dutch Colonial Revival style, 35, 66, 71, 73, 77, 104, 116, 121, 123

Edgar, Courtland V., 69

Eastlake style, 32, 68

Eastlake, Charles L., 32

Edbrook, F. E., 25, 88

Edwardian style (see also Free Classic), 31, 96, 111, 119, 120, 122, 123, 126

El Parque Street, 52, 53

El Paso Canal, 84

El Paso County Judicial Building, 54

El Paso Ice & Coal Company, 120

El Paso National Bank, 88

El Pomar Foundation, 86

Elizabethan style, 36, 82, 91

Elkton Consolidated Mining and Milling Company, 119

Elliot, David, 97

Elliot, Estella, 135

Elliot, E. V., 135

Elmslie, Constance, 52

Elmslie, William, 52

Emery, Bertha, 112

Emery, Charles, 112

Engleking, Otto, 50

Ensign, Edgar, 121

Ensign, Lilla, 121

Espanola Street, 100, 116, 118

Eubank, James J., 127

Evergreen Cemetery, 84

Exchange National Bank, 49, 86

F. S. Tucker Furniture Company, 117

Federal style, 35

Fire Station No. 1, 51

Fire Station No. 2, 131

First Christian Church, 54

First Congregational Church, 73

First Federal Savings and Loan Association, 48

First Lutheran Church, 89

First National Bank of Colorado Springs, 76, 78, 86, 88, 121, 134

First United Methodist Church, 54

Fish, Helen, 73

Fish, William, 73

Florio, Ernest, 56

Flower carnival, 73, 74, 83

Foard Brothers, 56

Foard, Roy, 56

Foard, Ruth, 56

Fontanero Street, 19, 24, 45, 52

Fort Carson, 18

Fountain Creek, 84

Frantz, Edna, 118

Frantz, J. Harold, 118

Free Classic (see also Edwardian style), 31, 96, 111, 119, 120, 122, 123, 126

Freed, Elaine, 20

French Eclectic style, 37, 56

Friedline, Justus R., 71

Funk, F. E., 134

Funk, Grace, 134

Gable End Frame, 34, 66, 67, 74, 98, 99, 105, 107, 114

Gamer, Carlton, 105

Garden of the Gods, 9, 74

Gatterer, George, 135

Gatterer, Nora, 135

Gem Toilet & Laundry, 131

Georgian style, 35, 44

Giddings Department Store, 89

Giddings, Ralph, 89

Giles Mercantile Company, 117

Gilpin, Frank, 79

Gilpin, Laura, 79

Girl Scouts, 75

Glen Eyrie, 60, 87

Glockner Hospital (Sanatorium), 12, 50

Glockner, Albert, 12

Glockner, Marie, 12

Gold, 10, 11, 17, 77, 78

Gold boom, 10, 11, 17

Gold Camp Road, 68

Gold mining, 10, 11, 17, 77, 78, 116

Goodson, Alice, 56

Goodson, Harry C., 56

Gove & Walsh, 89

Grand Junction & Grand River Valley Falls Railway Co., 70

Gray, Mary, 102

Gray, William L., 102

Great Depression, 15

Gregory, Anne, 115

Guzman, William A., 69

H. J. Newman & Company, 119

Hager, Clarissa, 83

Hager, Wilfrid, 83

Hagerman Peak, 64

Hagerman, James J., 64

Hagerman, Percy, 64

Half-timbered, 31, 113

Hamp, Linda, 75

Hamp, Josephine, 67

Hamp, Julia, 75

Hamp, Sidford, 67

Hamp, W. Francis, 75

Harden, Katherine, 132

Harden, Roy, 132

Harmon, Harold C., 130

Harmon, John, 78

Harmon, Mary B., 130

Harris, Ira, 98

Hassell Iron Works, 65, 66

Hassell, W. Bradford, 65

Hassell, William. W., 65, 66

Hayes, Varina Howell Davis, 106

Hazlett, Helen, 57

Hazlett, William L., 57

Heizer, David N., 66

Hemenway, Addie, 111

Hemenway, Alvaro, 111

Hemenway, O. E., 111

Hemming, C. C., 88

Hendee family, 60

Henry LeB. Wills & Company, 90, 92

Hetherington, T. D., 51, 121, 127, 128

Hibbard and Company, 60

Hibbard, Cassius A., 60

Historic preservation overlay zoning, 21

Holland, Rush L., 99

Holly Sugar Company, 49, 73

Holman, A. D. W., 110

Holman, H. V., 131

Holman, Julia, 110

Home Market Company, 132

Honeyman & Auld, 72

Honeyman, Mrs. W. J., 127

Hopkins, Berne, 53, 70

Horn, Chester B., 117

Horn, Frances, 117

Housing shortage, 18

Howard, Glenn, 110

Howard, Lester, 110

Howbert, Charles W., 100

Howbert, Mary, 100

Hoyt, Austin, 99

Independence Lode, 123

Industrial revolution, 43

Ingraham, Elizabeth Wright, 57

International style, 45, 52

Isabella Mining Company, 77, 89

Italian Renaissance Revival style, 39, 61, 88, 89

Italianate style, 29, 39, 102

Jackson, Harry, 48

Jacobean style, 36, 86

Jerome Hotel, 88

Jewett, Patty, 51, 89

Jewett, William K., 89

Jonson, William, 130

Jordan, Frank C., 126

Kelsey, Floyd L., 57

Kennedy, John F., 99

Kent, Annie, 92

Kent, Edward W., 92

Kernochan, E. L., 79

Kinsley, Mabel, 126

Kinsley, Samuel, 126

Kurie, Charles W., 120

Kurie, Mary, 120

Lansing, Abbie T., 79

Lansing, Sarah M., 79

Lawson, Jack, 99

LeCrone, George M., 107

Lefkowsky, Benjamin, 90

Lennox, John, 122

Lennox, Martha, 122

Leslie, Lydia E., 50

Lipsey, Julia Hassell, 65

Loevy, Robert D., 20

Loire Valley, 104

Loomis, Philip, 48

Loomis, Sara, 48

Lowell School, 129

Lucas, Katherine, 116

MacLaren and Thomas (see also Thomas, Charles and MacLaren, Thomas), 53

MacLaren, Thomas, 25, 49, 50, 51, 67, 68, 70, 73, 87, 121, 128, 134, 138

Macy, Mary, 136

Macy, William, 136

Macy's Department Store, 88

Macy's Pharmacy, 136

Manning, Cassius R., 74

Manning, Kizzie, 74

Marker, Isaac, 126

Marker, Lulu, 126

Marshall, Andrew, 75

Masonic Temple, 54

McClung, W. E., 85

McColl, Alex, 85

McColl, Rosie, 85

McCrossin, Leonora, 54

McCrossin, William P., 54

McGregor Hall, 128

McKay, L., 85

Medians, 16, 17, 23, 27

Memorial Hospital, 49, 113

Midland Bean Company, 53

Midland Railroad, 65

Mierow, Bernadine, 118

Mierow, Charles C., 118

Mies van der Rohe, Ludwig, 52

Miller, J. K., 123

Millionaire's Row, 17, 77

Mining Exchange, 74

Mollie Gibson Mining Company, 60, 64, 88

Monument Creek, 13, 15

Monument Valley Park, 13, 14, 18, 19, 24, 25, 46, 47, 66, 87

Morley, Frederick H., 76

Morse, Annie, 112

Morse, Ira J., 112

Moseley, Augustus, 126

Moseley, Zella, 126

Mulloy, M. E., 88

Munger, Dave, 21

Museum of Modern Art, 45

Myron Stratton Home, 113

Nathan, H. J., 131

Nathan, Minnie, 131

Nathan's Clothing Store, 131

National Register Historic District, 20

National Tuberculosis Association, 106

Neiman, E. E., 85

Nelson, J. Mark, 21

Neoclassical style, 38, 83

Nevada Avenue, 3, 14-16, 18, 19, 21, 24, 27, 30, 31, 42, 84, 102, 108, 109-123, 129, 138

New York Life Insurance Company, 85

Newman, Alice, 119

Newman, Harry J., 119

Newton Lumber Company, 85

Nicoll Warehouse Company, 48

Nicoll, Gladys, 48

Nicoll, William, 48

O'Brien, William, 60

O'Rourke, Dennis, 73

Old Colorado City, 9, 84

Old North End, 7, 9-21, 23-27, 30, 44, 51, 63, 65, 66, 84, 101, 106, 128, 138

Old North End Neighborhood (ONEN), 7, 19, 101, 138

Olson, Chastine, 54

Olson, O. Donald, 49

ONEN Plaque Program, 101

Orton, Charles, 55

Orton, Jospehine, 55

Palmer Hall, 14

Palmer High School, 54, 126

Palmer, William Jackson, 9-11, 13-16, 50, 60, 68, 84, 87

Parker, Asa W., 73

Parker, Octavia Bell, 78

Pattison, P. K., 122

Patty Jewett Golf Course, 51, 89

Pease & Barber, 123

Penrose Hospital, 12, 19, 50

Penrose, Spencer, 93

Perkins, Emily, 107

Perkins, Pliny, 72

Perkins, W. Arthur, 107

Perkins-Shearer Company, 83, 107

Peterson Field, 18

Phi Delta Theta, 123

Philadelphia Centennial, 35

Pikes Peak, 9, 10

Pikes Peak Avenue, 10, 78, 102, 134

Platte Avenue, 15

Portland Mill, 116

Portland Mine, 77, 78

Postlewaite, William W., 68

Prairie style, 42, 49, 117, 122

Preston, Elizabeth, 61

Preston, R. J., 61

Price, George Bacon, 100

Pulitzer, Joseph, 52

Queen Anne style, 30, 31, 33, 34, 44, 69, 72, 89, 96, 98, 102, 105, 111-113, 118, 119, 120, 122, 123, 126, 129

Railey, Matt, 101

Ranney, William W., 73

Reinitz, Beverly, 19

Rhea, Robert, 121

Richards, W. F., 92

Risher, Etta, 135

Risher, William, 135

Ritter, Etienne A., 114

Robert E. Lee Mine, 100

Roberts, Milnora, 64

Robinson, E. C. G., 83, 86, 93

Robinson, Charles Mulford, 16

Rock Island Railroad, 67

Rocky Mountains, 11, 12

Roeschlaub, Robert S., 128

Roosevelt, Theodore, 61

Root & Orton, 55

Royal Academy of Arts, 51

Ruhtenberg, Jan, 52

Russ-Amer Arms Apartments, 90

Russell Gates Mercantile Company, 127

Russell Produce Company, 71

Sadie's House, 101

San Miguel Street, 110, 125, 131

Sanitary Baking Company, 137

Sawyer, William J., 89

Schmitt, R. F., 126

Scholz, Samuel, 117

Scofield, Frances, 116

Scofield, Roger, 116

Searby, Mrs. F. W., 56

Seldomridge Bros., 82

Seldomridge, C. B., 82

Sharp, Arthur, 86

Sharp, Louise, 86

Shaw, Ruth, 19

Shearer, J. P., 83

Shields, Edna, 49

Shields, George K., 49

Shields, John G., 86

Shields-Morley Grocery Company, 76, 86

Shingle style, 33, 48, 60, 64, 67, 71, 73, 75, 82, 86, 88, 92, 111, 112, 116, 117, 120, 127

Shotwell, L. D., 57

Shove Memorial Chapel, 75

Shove, Eugene P., 75

Shove-Hager & Company, 75

Sidewalks, 17, 66, 84

Sierra Madre Street, 65

Simkins, Amanda, 129

Simkins, Emma, 129

Simkins, William, 129

Simpson, Adele, 53

Simpson, Fred, 53

Simpson Grain Company, 53

Sinton, W. K., 96

Sisters of Charity of Cincinnati, 12

Skinner, Lewis B., 130

Skinner, Olive, 130

Slocum, William Frederick, 14

Smith, Alex, 71

Smith, Amanda, 71

Smithsonian Institution, 138

Snyder, Jane, 52

Snyder, Maurice, 52

South Junior High School, 110

Spanish Colonial Revival style, 41, 49, 50, 55, 56, 87, 131

Spanish Mission style, 40, 41, 54, 55, 113

Sparks, Barbara, 20

Star and Crescent Creamery, 71

Star Laundry, 99

St. Francis Hospital, 49

St. Stephens Episcopal Church, 51

Steele School, 51, 138

Steele, Benjamin W., 138

Sterner, Frederick J., 25, 76

Stewart, Philip B., 61

Stewart, Sarah, 61

Stokes-Kernochan Insurance Agency, 79

Stote, Florence, 129

Stote, W. H. R., 129

Strachan, Florence, 134

Strachan, James, 134

Strachan, Jessie, 113

Strachan, William, 113

Stratton, F. E., 132

Stratton, Winfield Scott, 113

Streetcars, 14, 15

Streetlights, 17, 21

Strickler, David P., 113

Sunnyrest Sanatorium, 50

Szymanski, Jean, 19

Taylor, Alice Bemis, 62, 63

Taylor, Frederick, 62, 63

Taylor Hall, 63

Tejon Street, 14, 15, 21, 24, 29, 48, 60, 84, 89, 92-99, 101-107

Thomas, Charles E., 25, 51, 55

Thrall, Frank G., 110

Thrall, Louisa M., 110

Ticknor Hall, 128

Timmons, Merle H., 54

Traffic, 15, 18, 19, 21

Trolley, 14, 15

Tuberculosis, 12, 26, 50-52, 65, 71, 83, 105, 106, 115

Tucker, Fred, 117

Tucker, Mary, 117

Tudor style, 36, 39, 44, 48, 49, 56, 57, 62, 70, 85, 87, 114, 120, 121

Turnbull, G. B., 113

Tutt Alumni House, 93

Tutt, Charles L., 93

Tuttle, William H., 83

Twilley, William S., 68

Twilley, Cora, 68

Ullrich, Edgar, 120

Ullrich, Lulu, 120

Uintah Street, 7, 11, 14, 15, 17, 59, 81, 84, 95, 109, 115, 125

University of Colorado, 71, 106

University of Edinburgh, 128

Utah Copper Company, 93

Utah Ice and Storage Company, 120

Van Briggle Memorial Pottery, 115

Van Briggle Pottery Company, 49, 114, 115

Van Briggle, Anne, 114, 115

Van Briggle, Artus, 114, 115

Van den Arend, Nicholas, 25, 86, 115

Van Diest, E. C., 13, 87

Varian & Sterner (see also Sterner, Frederick), 61

Vassar College, 63

Victor, 10, 11, 12, 17, 123

W. R. Roby Lumber Company, 64

Wahsatch Avenue, 16-18, 20, 43, 44, 84, 124, 125, 129, 132-137

Wandell and Lowe Transfer and Storage Company, 103

Wandell, H. V., 103

Wandell, Lillie, 103

Wardwell, Gladys, 103

Wardwell, Robert, 103

Waring, James J., 71

Warren, Edward, 72

Warren, Ella, 72

Warren, Sarah, 72

Watt, Henry C., 50

Watt, Marjorie, 50

Webb, Gerald, 52, 71, 105, 106

Webb-Waring Institute for Medical research, 71, 106

Weber Street, 18, 20, 84, 124-127, 129-131, 138

Wendelken, Ben, 49

Wendelken, Mary, 49

Wheeler, Hattie H., 127

Wheeler, Jerome B., 88

Wiley, Alexander, 103

Wiley, Roxie, 103

Williams, Fred J., 96

Williams, Nelson B., 77, 89

Willis, Annie, 122

Willis, Willet R., 122

Wills, Caroline, 90

Wills, Henry LeB., 90

Wilson, Alice, 114

Wilson, George, 114

Wilson, Henry L., 96

Woestman, Edward F., 123

Woestman, Henrietta, 123

Womack, Robert, 10

Wood Avenue, 15-17, 24, 39, 47, 53, 58-64, 66-73, 75-79, 84

Wood, D. Russ, 69

Woodward, Annie, 116

Woodward, Edwin C., 116

World War I, 39, 65

World War II, 18

Wright, Frank Lloyd, 42, 57

Wright, T. J., 113

Y.M.C.A., 48

Bibliography

Books:

Cafky, Morris, and John A. Haney, *Pike's Peak Trolleys*. Colorado Springs, CO: Century One Press, 1983.

Clapesattle, Helen, *Dr. Webb of Colorado Springs*. Boulder, CO: Colorado Associated University Press, 1984.

Finley, Judith Reid, ed. *The Century Chest Letters of 1901: A Colorado Springs Legacy*. Colorado Springs, CO: Colorado College, 2001.

Fisher, John S., *A Builder of The West: The Life of General William Jackson Palmer*. Caldwell, ID: Caxton Printers, 1939.

Freed, Elaine, *Modern at Mid-Century: The Early Fifties Houses of Ingraham and Ingraham*. Colorado Springs, CO: Hulbert Center for Southwestern Studies, Colorado College, 2003.

Gardner, Mark L., *In the Shadow of Pike's Peak: An Illustrated History of Colorado Springs*. Carlsbad, CA: Heritage Media Corp, 1999.

Hershey, Charlie Brown, *Colorado College: 1874-1949*. Colorado Springs, CO: Colorado College, 1952.

Loevy, Robert D., *Colorado College: A Place Of Learning, 1874-1999*. Colorado Springs, CO: Colorado College, 1999.

McAlester, Virginia, *A Field Guide to American Houses*. New York: Alfred A. Knopf, 2000.

Oldach, Denise R. W., *Here Lies Colorado Springs: Historical Figures Buried in Evergreen and Fairview Cemeteries*. Colorado Springs, CO: City of Colorado Springs, Evergreen and Fairview Cemeteries, 1995.

Ormes, Manly Dayton, *The Book of Colorado Springs*. Colorado Springs, CO: Dentan Printing Co., 1933.

Reid, Juan, *Colorado College: The First Century, 1874-1974*. Colorado Springs, CO: Colorado College, 1979.

Sprague, Marshall, *Newport in the Rockies: The Life and Good Times of Colorado Springs*. 4th rev. ed. Athens, OH: Swallow Press/Ohio University Press, 1987.

Walker, Lester, *American Homes: The Illustrated Encyclopedia of Domestic Architecture*. New York: Black Dog & Leventhal Publishers, 2002.

Williams, Lester L. *Fighting Fire in Colorado Springs*. Colorado Springs, CO: Academy Printing, 1992.

Wilson, Henry L., *The Bungalow Book*. Mineola, NY: Dover Publications, Inc., 2006.

Newspaper Articles:

Colorado Springs Evening Telegraph Index, 1894-1946. Special Collections, Penrose Library, Pikes Peak Library District, Colorado Springs, CO.

Colorado Springs Free Press Index, 1947-1970. Special Collections, Penrose Library, Pikes Peak Library District, Colorado Springs, CO.

Colorado Springs Gazette Index, 1872-Present. Special Collections, Penrose Library, Pikes Peak Library District, Colorado Springs, CO.

Darrel Pearson, "Tree City, USA," *Colorado Springs Gazette*, April 23, 2009, Your Hub (Central, etc.), p. 1.

"Long, Slow Look," *Colorado Springs Sun*, September 16, 1970, p. 20.

Palmer, William Jackson (memoir), *Colorado Springs Gazette*, August 3, 1896. Reprinted August 1923 and August 1926.

Philip S.Arkow, "Land Use Plan: Extension of Fontanero Spurs Loud Opposition," *Colorado Springs Sun*, September 11, 1970, p. 1.

"Planners To Study Urban Renewal, Land-Use Plan," *Colorado Springs Sun*, September 10, 1970, p. 11.

Scott Prater, "Planting Grows In Old North End," *Colorado Springs Gazette*, June 7, 2006, Slice (Northwest/Central), p. 2.

Periodicals:

Facts Magazine Index, 1897-1903. Colorado Springs, CO: The Consolidated Publishing Company. Special Collections, Penrose Library, Pikes Peak Library District, Colorado Springs, CO.

Mountain Sunshine: Colorado Springs and the Pikes Peak region, 1899-1902. Colorado Springs, CO: Published under the auspices of the Chamber of Commerce. Special Collections, Penrose Library, Pikes Peak Library District, Colorado Springs, CO.

Legal Documents:

Declaratory Judgement, *Mary Kyer, Ruth Shaw, et. al., vs. City of Colorado Springs*, February 19, 1974.

Inter-Office Memorandum, (Colorado Springs) City Attorney's Office, "Palmer Reversionary Interest Acquisition," January 20, 1977.

Stipulation, *Mary Kyer, Ruth Shaw, et. al., vs. City of Colorado Springs*, March 23,1977.

Oral Histories:

Reinitz, Beverly, Oral History Interview, July 21, 1978, Special Collections, Penrose Library, Pikes Peak Library District, Colorado Springs, CO.

Szymanski, Jean, Oral History Interview, July 21, 1978, Special Collections, Penrose Library, Pikes Peak Library District, Colorado Springs, CO.

Other Resources:

Abele, Deborah, Priscilla Kaufman, Donna Urbanowski, and Jean Messinger. "North Weber Street-Wahsatch Avenue Historic Residential District National Register Nomination." Historic Preservation Alliance, 1985.

Bluebook of Colorado Springs, Colorado City and Manitou. Colorado Springs: Blue Book Publishing Co., 1898.

"Design Guidelines for North Weber/Wahsatch Historic District." Main Street Design. City of Colorado Springs, 1990.

Directories of Colorado Springs, Manitou Springs and Colorado City.
Colorado Springs, CO: S. N. Francis.

El Paso County Building Permits, 1878-1974. Special Collections, Penrose
Library, Pikes Peak Library District, Colorado Springs, CO.

Files of the Colorado Springs Landmarks Committee, Penrose Library Special
Collections, Colorado Springs, CO.

Freed, Elaine. "Colorado Springs Historic Ironwork." Pamphlet published
by Springs Area Beautiful Association and Pikes Peak or Bust Bicentennial
Committee, Colorado Springs, CO, 1976.

Freed, Elaine. "North End Historic District National Register Nomination."
Preservation Services, 1982.

Giles City Directories of Colorado Springs, Colorado City and Manitou.
Colorado Springs, CO: Giles Directory Company.

Nelson, J. Mark and Deborah Edge Abele "North End Historic District Design
Guidelines." Rev. 2nd ed. City of Colorado Springs, 1995.

*R. L. Polk & Co.'s Colorado Springs, Colorado City and Manitou City
Directories.* Colorado Springs, CO: R. L. Polk.

Sanborn Insurance Maps of Colorado Springs. The Sanborn Map Company,
New York, 1907, 1956.

Water Tapping Records of the City of Colorado Springs, 1902-1940. Special
Collections, Penrose Library, Pikes Peak Library District, Colorado Springs,
CO.

MAP OF THE OLD NORTH END NEIGHBORHOOD